Beyond Booked Solid reveals the secret to earning more and working less—leverage. And it's probably not what you think. Port has done it again. Simply brilliant.

—Barry Moltz, Entrepreneur and author of *Bounce!*

Beyond Booked Solid succeeds on every level, combining inspiring stories of real-life business owners with philosophical insights and the highest level strategic thinking—all wrapped up in a great "how-to" framework. This is a must-read for anyone wishing to achieve entrepreneurial success and personal fulfillment at the same time.

—Sandra Yancey, Founder and CEO, eWomenNetwork, Inc.

Michael Port has done it again! With a simple process that can apply to almost any business, he provides a blueprint for taking your business to the next level—where you can work less and accomplish more. If your business is successful, but only with your constant supervision, rush out and buy this book.

—Marci Alboher, Author of "One Person/Multiple Careers & Columnist," *The New York Times*

Contrary to what Donald Trump says, bigger is not always better. Instead, wouldn't you rather make more money and work less? You can with *Beyond Booked Solid*. Port offers a remarkable system for innovating in your business that is the key to doing less and accomplishing more. Highly recommended.

—Aaron Altscher, Owner of Altscher Marketing Consulting and NBC's *The Apprentice,* LA

Every once in a long while, a book comes along that stands head and shoulders above the rest and sets a new standard. This is one of those rare books. When you're ready to demolish the invisible barriers between yourself and massive success—and transform your business as well as your life—read this book.

—Frank Rumbauskas, *New York Times* bestselling author of *Never Cold Call*

Beyond Booked Solid is a must-read for those striving to understand the changing environment that we live and work in. You will learn that abundant living comes from a balance between working hard and letting go. This book will teach you what that really means. It will also give you essential insights that will take you from average results to massive success in business and in life. Read this one with pen in hand and get ready to learn something big.

—Kody Bateman, Founder and CEO, SendOutCards

BEYOND
BOOKED
SOLID

Your Business, Your Life,
Your Way—It's All Inside

MICHAEL PORT

John Wiley & Sons, Inc.

Published by John Wiley & Sons, Inc., Hoboken, New Jersey.
Published simultaneously in Canada.

For general information on our other products and services or for technical support, please contact our Customer Care Department within the United States at (800) 762-2974, outside the United States at (317) 572-3993 or fax (317) 572-4002.

Wiley also publishes its books in a variety of electronic formats. Some content that appears in print may not be available in electronic books. For more information about Wiley products, visit our web site at www.wiley.com.

Special thanks to Hal Macomber for his insight and contribution to this work. Without the use of his intellectual property and generous time, this book couldn't have been written.

Library of Congress Cataloging-in-Publication Data:

Port, Michael, 1970–
    Beyond booked solid : your business, your life, your way—it's all inside/Michael Port.
      p. cm.
    Includes bibliographical references and index.
    ISBN 978-0-470-17436-4 (cloth)
      1. Small business—management. 2. Creative ability in business. 3. Strategic planning. 4. Business planning. I. Title.
    HD62.7.P675   2008
    658.4'068—dc22
                                                      2007043558

Printed in the United States of America.

10 9 8 7 6 5 4 3 2 1

To David Port, MD,
George Lyons Sensei, and Hal Macomber . . .
for opening my eyes to the pursuit of mastery.

Contents

Acknowledgments

Mina Samuels, meeting you and working with you has been the birthday present of the decade. Actually, that may be an understatement. Hal Macomber, for your invaluable contributions to this work and for your friendship, leadership, and mentorship. I remember the first time I met you. I liked you as much then as I do now. Gayla DeHart for challenging me to write this book and for helping me to conceive it. You are an inspiration. I hang on every word you say. Elizabeth Marshall, for your intelligence and talent. Yale definitely does not want their degree back. Kathryn Green, every writer should be so lucky to have an agent like you . . . and an editor like Matt Holt. Amy Ewart, you and your team deserve more than thanks for managing me (and my business), not to mention for overlooking my unusual expectations and impatience. Oh, and for coming up with the title of the book. Gosh, what don't you do? Kody Bateman, Dr. Mike Berkley, Brandon Hartsell, Jonathan Hunt, Lori Kliman, Ron Quintero, Brian Scudamore, and Heather White for sharing your stories. I hope I did you justice. Bob D'Amico (who did the illustrations for this book), you are a consummate professional. Kevin McAleer (who designed the process maps), you are a perfectionist of the best kind. Peter Hurley (who took the picture for the cover), you may just be the best photographer in the world. Asking others to read early drafts of a manuscript is asking a lot, so many thanks to those who took the time, like Shannon Vargo, Cara Lumen, Bea Fields, and Iva Peele. The members of Bucks County Aikido for practicing with me. *Domo arigato-gozaimashita.* Of course, Mom and Dad, none of this would be possible without you two. I love you very much. Shannon, your book is next. It will change the world.

Preface

The significant problems we have cannot be solved at the same level of thinking with which we created them.
—Albert Einstein

As a seasoned professional, you know that for every problem you successfully overcome—such as needing more clients, the topic I focused on in my first book—another more challenging problem inevitably follows, such as how to grow your business when all of your time is booked with clients.

With every success comes new challenges, and this repeated cycle is a constant state of being for the entrepreneur. Each time we solve a problem, we begin a new game at a higher level, one in which we're facing new problems.

Most of our business problems are self-created because we've stepped up to a higher level of play. If you are willing to solve the problems you face, the sky is the limit. Each problem you confront in your business is just a bit bigger than your current capacity to handle it. Oh, I know sometimes it doesn't seem that way. Sometimes it seems like the problems we face are insurmountable, especially those that lead us into the unknown. That's why we need to solve our new problems with a more sophisticated level of thinking than the one that created the problems in the first place. If you can do that, you will continue to increase your capacity for doing bigger and better things in the world. That's what I try to do every day. Is it easy? No. Are there "three easy steps"? Doubtful. But is it worth it? Absolutely.

I will show you how to make more money *and* to work less on the things that you dislike, that frustrate you, or that you are simply not good at doing. I will show you how to turn a one-person operation into a highly successful enterprise that serves many more clients than you ever dreamed possible. That's what I mean when I say a "bigger, better business." It doesn't mean you work more (though you may have to in the very short term), and it doesn't even necessarily mean you end up with an office full of employees you have to manage. It means learning how to leverage what you're good at so you can afford to focus on what you love in your work and in the rest of your life. After all, it's your business and your life; you can and should run them your way.

Right now this may seem more like a dream than a possible reality. But as you shift your thinking and take action using the techniques and strategies this book, you will see that it is entirely possible to achieve your dream and that it can happen much faster than you ever imagined.

In *The Practice of Management*, Peter Drucker wrote, "Because the purpose of business is to create a customer, the business enterprise has two—and only two—basic functions: marketing and innovation. Marketing and innovation produce results; all the rest are costs."

My first book, *Book Yourself Solid: The Fastest, Easiest, and Most Reliable System for Getting More Clients Than You Can Handle Even if You Hate Marketing and Selling* (Wiley, 2006), was born out of the issues I faced as someone who wasn't comfortable with the typical marketing and sales mentality. I needed to create a marketing system that I could rely on to sustain my business. My approach works. On average, 90 percent of the people who fully implement the strategies I teach in the Book Yourself Solid 15-Week Group Coaching Program increase their revenues by over 40 percent within the first year of completing the program. *Book Yourself Solid* addressed the first basic function of a business as identified by Drucker.

This book, *Beyond Booked Solid,* was born out of the challenges, problems, and struggles I have faced since writing *Book Yourself Solid.* Every word is based on the sweat, tears, laughter, and joy of building a bigger, better business that leverages the power of people and processes and generates more money while the business owner (who could be you!) works less.

In thinking about how to grow your businesses, do you find yourself in any of these situations?

- You feel trapped into providing one-on-one services and are unable to leverage your time to explore ways to generate multiple revenue streams.
- You have lots of great ideas, but lack the wherewithal to implement them.
- You believe that your business will suffer if other people serve your clients because you are the only one who can deliver your services.
- You worry about your people and project management skills because you spend precious time hiring and training due to staff turnover (time that could be better spent on growing your business).
- You think you ought to fly solo without truly understanding the need for a strong network of support, both personally and professionally.
- You know that you lack the right systems or procedures to support the ongoing business development, marketing, and administrative activities of the business. As you get busier, you stop marketing and find that your business becomes inconsistent; or you get bogged down with paperwork and end up staying at the office several hours later than you intended.
- You lack the right tools to forecast and budget effectively, so you're constantly worried about where the next dollar is coming from. You end up making financial decisions without really understanding the implications.

- You have trouble incorporating work/life balance. There's never enough time for family and friends, exercise, hobbies, travel, and all the other things you keep promising yourself you'll do . . . when you have the time.

If you identify with any of these issues, you're in the right place. I can help you approach your business from a new and inspired perspective so you can focus first on serving your clients and then on growing your business.

This book, *Beyond Booked Solid,* focuses on what Peter Drucker identified as the second basic function of your business—innovation. It will help you discover your capacity to innovate in your business, through creativity and systems thinking, so you can make the changes necessary in your business to go beyond booked solid.

This book gives you the strategies, techniques, and tips you need to build a bigger, better business. It will inspire you to take action and help you stay accountable so you build the business that's best for you. And by the way, growth (a bigger, better business) can mean many things—bigger revenues, bigger profits, bigger operations. It's up to you what it will mean in your business. Growth is a very different challenge from booking yourself solid.

You may have read my first book, *Book Yourself Solid.* However, it's certainly not a necessary prerequisite. No matter what stage of business development you're in, you can benefit from the methods you'll find in this book. But if you aren't booked solid yet, you may want to go back and read *Book Yourself Solid,* too. If you have read it, then you're familiar with its step-by-step process and sequential exercises. Each chapter builds on the previous chapter and requires that you work through everything up to that point.

Don't do that with this book! Unlike booking yourself solid, going beyond booked solid is not a matter of steps 1–2–3. It is not a matter of picking off a menu. Building a bigger, better business is an organic, iterative, and ongoing process. You can't dabble. Nor can you obsess.

If you try a little of this from here and a little of that from there, you will not reach your goal. However, if you obsess over perfection, don't start until all of your ducks are in a row, try to do everything all at once, or never let anything go because it's not quite perfect enough, you won't reach your goal either.

Read this book all the way through. You need to see what the whole process is first. This will help to create an open space in your mind, to think about where you want to go and how you want to get there. Once you are thinking about your objectives, you can go back and work through the process (*master* the process), applying what you have learned. The process of mastery is like beginning an apprenticeship. The changes to your business (and to yourself) are not going to happen all at once, but they will happen. What's inside this book may change what's inside you. You may discover your untapped capacity to do great things in the world.

This book is about what Timothy Ferriss, author of *The 4-Hour Workweek,* calls "elegance," the balance between dabbling and obsessing that enables you to build your business—without losing yourself. You *can* run your business, and your life, in *your* way. It's what I call *mastery*—the focus and the application you need to excel at something. The book is not so much a workbook—though it has that element—as it is a book that will guide you to a new way of seeing your business and taking action to change it. This book is about finding new ways of being. As I said, read through the book once. Then read through it again and start building your bigger, better business . . . and pursue mastery.

In *Beyond Booked Solid,* we'll look at *how* and *why* some small business owners make the leap and build a bigger, better business and others don't. The *how* are the practical, brass tacks things you can do to grow your business—the action steps you can take, such as designing a better structure and putting the right systems in place. The *why* are the ways you need to think and be, to innovate, to collaborate, and to complete the projects you will have to do to achieve your objectives;

it is being successful from the inside out. I think of it this way—*how* is doing; w*hy* is being.

In *Beyond Booked Solid,* we'll decide the scope of the change you want to make now that you're booked solid—because being booked solid isn't all that it's cracked up to be, is it? Then we'll investigate a variety of business building blocks with which you can create a better, more leveraged, business architecture for the future, so you really can earn more money while working less. And, finally, we'll reconceive your business structure to go beyond booked solid.

What do I mean by *business architecture?* The architecture of your business is *how* you do business and it is *how* you will grow. It is what Hal Macomber, cofounder of Lean Project Consulting, Inc., and an important contributor to this book, calls the *structures for fulfillment* in your business. It is how you create and deliver your product or service. A better architecture may include outsourcing busywork, systematizing operations, producing projects, exploring opportunities for passive revenue, and leveraging your marketing efforts so that you are able to work creatively on building the business, have more free time, and, ultimately, think bigger about who you are and what you have to offer the world. To go beyond booked solid, you will need to think more consciously about your architecture and likely do some restructuring.

As we are delving into the action steps you will take, we'll also rediscover the power of ongoing innovation in our businesses—*why* you will succeed. We'll set goals for the future and get there. We'll master the art of the project and how to work with others. We'll explore the fine points of collaborating, cooperating, and delegating to get things done because your business will grow faster when others do it with you and for you.

Finally, we'll look at *how* to put your operations on autopilot to save your sanity and to give you freedom. We'll find the delicate balance between people and processes—how to get great people to execute great processes so that your business virtually runs itself.

Breakdown is inevitable, so we'll learn how to protect against the repercussions and get the train back on the tracks. We'll also, for once and for all, finally achieve a work/life balance, because ultimately this balance is at the heart of *why* you can be someone who serves others as you serve your destiny.

Here's a sneak preview of what's inside:

- The four criteria necessary to build a business that takes you beyond booked solid: profitability, scalability, excellence, and leverage
- How to innovate in your business
- How to cultivate the right attitude for success (this is not only about being positive)
- How to reduce the hours you work and make more money
- How to work with people inside and outside your business
- How to complete remarkable projects
- How to expand the business into a bigger operation and leverage being booked solid, potentially doubling, tripling, and even quadrupling sales within the first year
- How to find opportunities for earning passive and leveraged revenue
- How to systematize all areas of the business so the business runs without the business owner (that's you)
- How to cost-effectively delegate virtually all administrative and busywork to others—without necessarily having more employees
- How to prioritize tasks and projects to make sure things get done
- How to, once and for all, consistently take time off to "sharpen the saw" and increase your creativity
- How to balance the demands of work with a rich personal life

Throughout the book, I'll refer to a number of entrepreneurs, using their experiences as real-work examples. You may be itching to know their whole stories, and you will. In the final chapter, we'll look at how real people have built bigger, better businesses, their successes, and what we can learn from their mistakes.

I have had to dig very deep to grow my business from a training and consulting business, in which I was fully responsible for every function of the business, from bookkeeping to booking appointments, from Web site design to window washing, from lead generation to licking envelopes, and every other detail of running a one-person business. I'm sure you know this scene well.

Fortunately, I've been able to turn the corner. Where I was once able to serve no more than 30 clients a month, I now serve an average of 500 clients a month in my intensive coaching programs and thousands more every month through my books and CD programs, live events, and keynote addresses all over the world. I have redesigned the business to support as many clients as I choose—with no limit on the number I can serve.

If you are willing to dig down to the roots of your problems, rather than just hacking at the leaves, then the process revealed in the pages of this book can help you grow a formidable business that will yield fruit for years to come. Your business, your life, your way—it's all inside.

Read on and experience the results. And remember, read once and absorb, then read again and take action.

The book includes written exercises that will support you in the process. You'll want to retain your responses to the written exercises for regular review and, of course, for implementation. I have also prepared a free downloadable Beyond Booked Solid (BBS) Toolkit that includes additional resource and support materials, including the essential BBS Report. Simply visit my Web site and download the Toolkit before you get started.

Go to www.BeyondBookedSolid.com right now and download your free copy of the BBS Toolkit before you turn another page.

At the Web site, you'll also find my blog that builds on what's in all of my books. It's a place you can ask questions and comment on what I'm doing or how you're doing.

Although you'll no doubt get great value just from reading this book, the real value—along with your success—lies in your decision to take an active role by tapping into your creativity, doing the exercises, adjusting your perspective, making changes in your business, and learning new ways of being. You will continue an evolutionary journey of personal and business development that will empower you to achieve the success you know you're capable of attaining.

Come to *Beyond Booked Solid* with an open heart and mind. Set aside any preconceived notions of what it means to build a bigger, better business—the way you've seen it done, or think it should be done, may not actually be the best path for you. Inside is an opportunity to create a new and inspired way of working. You will find creative and profit-producing advice for eliminating the feeling of being overwhelmed and for avoiding feelings of frustration and isolation. Let your future reveal itself—day by day. Let me lead you to a business booked solid with high-paying clients, a business that will continue to grow (and grow and grow) and allow you to work less (and less and less).

I hope that your journey to a bigger, better business is filled with abundance, meaning, and joy. I am honored to walk next to you on this path. I know that your breakthrough to even greater success is near and that you will continue to sustain that success through your faith in yourself, your inner strength, and your confidence.

As significant personal or professional questions come up, please get in touch with me. I'm always delighted to hear from you and to have the opportunity to help. You can reach me at questions@michaelport.com.

Ready to go beyond booked solid? Let's do it!

1

How and Why—
Doing and Being

In all living there is a certain narrowness of application which leads to breadth of power. We have to concentrate on a thing in order to master it. Then we must be broad enough not to be narrowed by our specialties.

—Ralf W. Sockman

So you want to go beyond booked solid? Great. Now what? Before we plunge in, let's understand the framework of our future success— what I call the *how* and the *why: how* we will build a bigger, better business and *why* we will achieve our objective.

Going beyond booked solid means working *on* your business. *E-Myth* author Michael E. Gerber best describes this idea of working *on* your business while working *in* your business. Working *in* your business is making sure the service or the product you offer to the market is as good as it can be. You've successfully figured out how best to work *in* your business. That's why you're booked solid. Now you need to work *on* your business. Working *on* your business refers to the improvements you can make in everything from how you approach your business, to how it's structured, to the systems you have in place

1

to help you run the business. There's a catch: You can't just stop working *in* your business to focus *on* the business. *You need to work "on" your business, while working "in" your business.* This allows you to make money and to get real-time results at the same time. It helps you to create, produce, and sustain your business faster. It is *how* you will succeed.

However, it's not enough to work *in* and *on* your business. To that, let's add *while working on yourself.* Your business is a reflection of who you are and what you can handle. And, of course, the real bottom line is your life—and enjoyment of it. You can work all you want, but if in the end you are dissatisfied with your life, unfulfilled, and alienated from your family and friends because you never see them, what's the point? As we work through this book, keep in mind what it's all for. It's important to stay tuned in to your needs from the beginning. *Working on yourself* is about more than just your personal well-being. It's about your professional and business well-being, too. It's about having your business, and your life, your way. It is *why* you will succeed. It is why you will be able to absorb and to implement the extraordinary amount of content—tools, methods, and strategies to build your business—that you will find in these pages.

Where to start? That's a question that can stop a project cold. You might feel overwhelmed by the number of things you can list right off the top of your head to do to work *on* your business, not to mention all the work you have to do *in* it. Then I come along with this book and suggest, for example, that you design a new architecture for your business. And that's just one piece of *how* you will work *on* your business. But showing you *how* to work on your business is not enough. I will also show you *why* some people succeed and others don't. *Why?* To go beyond booked solid, you'll need to learn how to let go of some of your old ideas and get creative in your business—innovate. This innovation process requires you to open yourself up to new ideas, to find new ways of being—that's why I call it *working on yourself.*

Innovation

Maybe you're thinking, "It's business. What's this about opening up?" Here's why. Creating and sustaining a business at a new, higher level requires innovation. Without innovation, your ideas, the new business architecture you'll design, will stay just that—ideas and dreams. Innovation starts with you. Every successful entrepreneur, indeed every successful person, is an innovator. You might be saying to yourself, "Not me, I'll never invent the lightbulb." Don't confuse the idea of innovation with the idea of invention. Innovation is an inward- and outward-looking process. It is an essential part of the process of self-actualization or the pursuit of mastery, a concept I think is vital to success.

An innovator can change perspective and adopt new habits. Innovation is changing the way you do and see things. It is asking yourself, "How will I view my business differently today than I did yesterday?" I know you're ready to do that because you're reading this book. Of course, it is possible to shift perspective without taking deliberate action. We're going to do more than that. We are going to develop new perspectives (that's *why* this approach works) and then adopt new goals and new practices to reach those goals (that's *how* this approach works).

For many people, innovation can be overwhelming. It can be scary. We can feel trapped by our business, stuck in habits, practices, and perspectives. "I conduct seminars," you might think. The idea of webinars or monthly newsletters may seem beyond your reach. You feel safe with your present practices. I know. I've been there. I still am, because it's not a one-shot deal. You can't innovate and be done with it. Innovation, building a bigger, better business, is an organic process, iterative and ongoing. Every time you solve a problem or meet a challenge, a new one presents itself. It is a process of creation, maintenance, and destruction followed by re-creation and so on. It's very rare to be able to dust off your hands and say, "Now then, I'm done."

Hal Macomber, whose insight was invaluable to this book, likes to use the orange juice carton example to illustrate this cycle of innovation. For a long time, orange juice was sold in cardboard cartons with cardboard spouts. But orange juice in this form (i.e., not frozen concentrate) didn't last very long. So something had to be done to give the orange juice longer shelf life. Pasteurization turned out to be the answer, which was great, except for one thing: Orange juice (which is a long-lasting acid liquid) degraded the cardboard spout. One challenge solved, another presented. Something had to be done, or the paperboard industry couldn't supply cartons to the orange juice producers anymore. The next innovation was the plastic spout on the cardboard juice container. Great, again. Of course, the plastic spout likely brought its own new challenges, but we won't get into those. As each new hurdle is overcome, another presents itself. And the cycle repeats again and again.

If you want to go beyond booked solid, you'll need to take the plunge and become an innovator. I'll show you that it's not nearly as daunting as it seems. In fact, it can and should be exhilarating, which is not to say it won't be hard work—it will be, but that's okay because in the end you'll be earning more and working less, and the process of innovation will continue. On top of that, you'll be experiencing the deep sense of purpose that comes from the pursuit of mastery.

What does it really mean to *innovate*? Divesting the busywork that takes up too much of your time, which would be better spent with your clients on your "real" work—that's innovating. Figuring out how to outsource the mechanisms for keeping in touch with clients through regular mailings or other contact—that's innovating. Implementing new record-keeping systems—that's innovating. Finding little ways to alleviate annoyances—that's innovating. Restructuring your business so it's built for growth, while at the same time lightening your load—that's innovating.

In fact, this whole book is about innovating—learning and developing new ways of doing things, and committing to mastery. Now that you're booked solid, what you want next is up to you. It's not just about choosing and implementing. It's not about becoming remarkable—because being able to keep a business afloat is a remarkable achievement in its own right. You've already done that and better. You're booked solid or on your way. Innovating is about being able to create a new story for your future without being trapped by your past. It means being someone who can simultaneously transcend their history to achieve goals well beyond their standard expectations, while at the same time respecting and incorporating the best of what they've learned from their past (being what's called *ahistorical*). This book suggests a way of engaging in the world that will keep you innovating, creating (and recreating) the business you want.

Real life is messy. Be prepared to leap ahead at points and circle back at others. You'll be cultivating your innovation skills at the same time that you're building your new architecture. You'll be implementing systems at the same time that you're choosing the right business building blocks. Your business, like life, is an always changing, dynamic enterprise. The most importantly thing might be flexibility. Like the tree that bends in the wind but doesn't break, you need to be open and resilient. It's a lifelong process. So, we'll talk, too, about how to stay on course. That said, here goes.

Where You Are

If you are booked solid, you are in one of two camps: Either you are pleased with the size of your business but would like to increase your fees, spend fewer hours working, and feel more confident using your Red Velvet Rope Policy (I talked about this policy in *Book Yourself Solid;* it is your filtration system that ensures you work with ideal clients who energize and inspire you and, most importantly, allow you to do your best work); or you want to significantly grow your business and serve many more people, open more locations, and hire more staff. In both cases what you will learn to do is leverage more so you work less. When I say "bigger," that can mean more profitable but not necessarily a larger operation. It's a matter of scope.

Your instinct might be to resist implementing the new ideas you'll find in these pages: you are not sure whether they will work, whether your customers will like them, or whether you can maintain the current business while building the new business. The changes to your business can't and won't happen overnight. You are already too busy. But it will happen. It might involve a change in attitude and a little extra work for a while, but the long-term payoff of working more efficiently will profoundly change your future. And that's what this book is about—your future.

Designing your business architecture is an ongoing process—the business is never complete, just as people are never complete. We are all a work in progress. Getting a degree, getting married, or starting your business may seem like end goals while you are working toward them, but they are really just starting points for the ever-evolving landscape of your life. Going beyond booked solid is committing to a life of mastery, always making changes and striving to improve.

Let's look at *how* you will grow a bigger, better business and *why* you will succeed.

2 | Decide—The Change You Want to Make

Nothing is more difficult, and therefore more precious, than to be able to decide.

—*Napoleon I*

You're booked solid. Now what?

Bigger is not always better, says Seth Godin, author of *Small Is the New Big*. And he may be right. What you are changing is the scope of your business. The scale may change, too, but it's not a requirement of moving beyond booked solid. Don't make assumptions regarding what you should do with your business. Even if you are perfectly clear on what you want to do, what I propose is that you consider multiple alternative structures for your emerging business. I'd like to help you choose your direction. I don't want you to end up at the top rung of the ladder only to realize that you've climbed to the wrong destination. The choices you make are critical. Now that you're booked solid, or are on your way, there's a great deal at stake. You have less time

7

to experiment and more expectations to meet based on promises that you've been making to your customers, associates, and partners (never mind promises you've made to family, friends, and yourself about where you want your life to be). This chapter offers a set of options to consider and to help you crystallize your vision and stoke your imagination. The actions you will ultimately take as a result of this thinking are a crucial part of *how* you will grow.

You may resist some of the suggestions or options. You may have preconceived notions and expectations that are limiting your growth. We all do. If you've believed something for a long time, it's understandable that you may reject an alternative belief or option without reflecting on it fully or experiencing the alternative. If it were easy to build a bigger, better business that leverages the power of people and processes, then everyone would do it at the earliest possible moment. When you feel yourself resisting, consider why you feel constrained. Is the constraint real or self-imposed (self-inflicted)?

I have found, and continue to find, this process challenging. Over time, many of my beliefs and assumptions have been shattered. I've gotten knocked off my feet by a wave, only to stand up and get knocked down again. But I know in my heart that character is built not by chance, but by the number of times I keep getting back up. I've come to see the entrepreneurial initiative as an opportunity to lose something every day—something holding me back—and in the process earn success.

I once heard it said that the only person who likes change is a baby with a dirty diaper. Change is such an extraordinary, sometimes uncomfortable thing, isn't it? So many of us crave it but fiercely resist it, fueling an ever-escalating inner civil war. In our society, we may have taken the privilege of comfort too far. It's so easy to stay comfortable. Too warm? Adjust the air-conditioning another degree cooler. Too cold now? Turn the heat up a few degrees. We insulate ourselves against anything that is the least bit uncomfortable. I'm not talking about the extreme discomfort of not having a roof over your head or of being the victim of abuse or some other horrible circumstances. I'm talking about the everyday entitlement that leads us to believe that everything we want should be handed to us, that mastery can be attained through a bit of dabbling or by short bursts of obsessive attention.

I believe the process that we go through in this book will be rewarding if you are willing to purposely create a certain amount of discomfort for yourself, your associates, and probably for your family and friends, too. You will become more comfortable with discomfort. Then big things will happen. The goal is not making changes simply for the sake of change, but rather for the sake of continuing to serve the people you're meant to serve and, at the same time, fulfill your destiny.

To help determine the best course of action for you, let's establish where you are now, and then let's see which of the two scenarios that follow best represents your situation.

Current State

You have a decent stable of clients who like (maybe love) you. You're making ends meet. You love working with your clients; spending time with them; and dealing with their issues, needs, and desires (but maybe not as much as you used to). You're relatively comfortable, except that you are spending a considerable—okay, a ridiculous— amount of time on stuff you hate doing and may not be very good at doing. You're missing time with your family and friends. You've all but forgotten that you once had hobbies. In fact, you don't have much of a life outside of work.

What would you rather do?

Build by Extension

Your desire: To keep working with your clients and maybe even spend more time with your clients. You're pleased with the amount of money you're making. Okay, maybe a little more would be nice, but you don't have the need or the desire to increase your revenues exponentially. Making gobs of money is not an obligation or some sort of mandate, by the way. It's not for everyone and is certainly not necessary to live a meaningful and purposeful life. What you really want is to work only with clients (not all the other business-running stuff), to be able to choose your ideal clients, and to work only with people who energize and inspire you. In other words, you want to do the work that you were meant to do and nothing else. You don't want to manage a big staff or open multiple locations or someday take your company public. For you, thinking big means being fully self-expressed in your work and your life. It doesn't necessarily mean that you need to grow a business that is bigger, size-wise. Doing big things in the world means that you're aligned with your purpose. You want to work with the fundamental business you have but do some renovations, maybe add a new wing, extend the structure in such a way that ensures that you are doing the best of the work you want to do, while the rest is taken care of by others.

One small caveat: If you identify with building by extension, in my experience, most people would play a bigger game in the world if they thought they could. So, even if you think that you want to do just what you're doing minus the busywork, might I suggest that you keep a small space in your consciousness open to the possibility that there are opportunities available to you that you have not yet considered? And, some of these opportunities may be attractive to you.

Build New

Your desire: You want to make much more money. And you'd like to work less. You want to build a business that is scalable, meaning it can grow exponentially, a business that either does not require that you continue to deliver all services or that enables you to serve 10 or 100 times more clients. You are excited by the idea of managing other people, possibly opening other locations or creating a business that can be licensed or franchised. You want to spend your time being more entrepreneurial, thinking about the big picture of your business and your life, instead of being mired in small details, like whether you need to order more envelopes. In fact, you may feel ready to move beyond the confines of the business you're in, something that can and likely will happen as your business grows. You want to build something not only bigger but also new.

Right now, make a commitment to change. Not sure yet what that change will be? That's perfectly fine, of course. I don't expect you to know yet. That's what this book is all about—helping you decide what changes to make. And if you think you already know, be patient. Read first. We're going to start by looking at your attitude—the mental place you need to be before you can make any successful changes. Being mentally prepared can be the difference between making the leap and standing still.

3

How Do You Feel about the Future?— Be Disposed toward Success

My future starts when I wake up every morning. . . . [E]very day I find something creative to do with my life.
—**Miles Davis**

Whether you want to build by extension or build new, both require the right psychological foundation. So how do you feel about working *on* your business (and *on yourself*)? I'm not just asking because I care about your well-being. This is a critical question. Your attitude, your disposition, your perspective, your mood (whatever you want to call it) about the future is a crucial factor in your success. What's inside—your inner resources—is as important as money, people, and all the other tangible resources you'll need to grow your business. You will not build a bigger, better business if you are not in the right mood. "Not tonight, I have a headache," has a similar effect in business as it does at home—nothing happens except frustration. It's not enough to know you want to build something new or extended. To succeed, you need to know why you're doing what you're doing.

What am I working toward in this business? Why am I pursuing this goal? There are no absolute right answers to these questions. We each have different ambitions that drive us. But your answer to these questions needs to be on top of mind as you move through this process. In fact, being able to sustain the right attitude may be the most important part in *why* you will succeed. I really mean that.

This business about your attitude may seem hokey or just so much intellectualizing, or philosophizing, or something. It's not. This is a crucial piece of the solution to the challenge of how to go beyond booked solid. You might even realize that philosophy can be fun (and, yes, practical).

Cultivate Curiosity

To innovate, you need to be curious. Yet, we all go through periods where we just don't want to take on something new, periods where we feel overwhelmed by the things we need to learn to move ahead with our projects and with our lives. How will you maintain your curiosity?

Dr. Mike Berkley wasn't always an acupuncturist and founder of the Berkley Center for Reproductive Wellness and Women's Health. He used to be a computer salesman. One day he read a story about a woman who stood in the middle of her town square, took her clothes off piece by piece, and gave them away to people who needed them. When her friends asked her what she was doing, she said, "All that is not given is lost." The message hit Mike in a powerful way— he couldn't stop thinking about it. He realized he was taking more than he was giving (not that being a computer salesman necessarily implies a lack of generosity). A few months later, he saw an ad for an acupuncture school opening in his area. He knew almost nothing about it, except what a friend who was an acupuncturist had told him—but he was curious. He went to the open house and ended up staying six years until he started his own practice. Now he's in a business that allows him to serve people every day. He was led there by his curiosity. He stays there because every day there's a reason to stay curious—so he can give more than he takes. (You can find Mike's full story, along with those of the other entrepreneurs I'll mention as we go along, in the Case Studies in Chapter 14.)

Be Ambitious

To build your business, you need to be ambitious. That goes without saying, but ambition is an energetic attitude. How will you maintain the energy of ambition?

Kody Bateman, CEO of SendOutCards.com, was told hundreds of times by "professionals, gurus, and consultants" in his industry that he couldn't do what he wanted. He wanted to start a company that helped people send cards to friends, family, and clients, a company that helped people respond to that fleeting inner voice that reminds them that they ought to be in touch with someone but that they usually ignore or forget about because it passes out of their minds so quickly. Kody knows about missed opportunities. In 1989, Kody didn't respond to an urge to take time to say a proper goodbye to his older brother when Kody was leaving for a job across the country. Three months later, his brother was killed. Kody doesn't want that kind of experience to happen again in his life, and he wants to help others avoid it, too. The "why" that inspired Kody's dream for the card-sending company was so big that it sustained him in the face of the naysayers and got him through to where he is today—CEO of the largest online greeting card company, one that in the future may give Hallmark and American Greetings a run for their money.

To succeed, you need people around you who support your ambition, who nurture your inner strength, and who cultivate and maintain curiosity as well. Staff, partners, family, friends, and others need to share in some sense your attitude and ambition. (After all, that's the foundation of what it is to be supportive as a friend, family member, or coworker, isn't it?) I'm going to offer this suggestion—don't use the Golden Rule (that we should treat others the way we want to be treated) when you are asking others to share your attitude and ambition. I'm going to suggest using what author Dr. Tony Alessandra has coined as the Platinum Rule: "Treat others the way they want to be treated." Quite a concept, yes? Reflect on it. Your success requires that people around you feel similarly disposed toward the future. This is not to say that they must want the exact same thing you do. Rather it means that they, too, have ambitions of their own, which coincide with or complement your own. Furthermore, they must be able to maintain their disposition toward the future. You want to build a bigger, better business; your team wants the opportunity to be part of a growing enterprise, to pursue their ambitions within your organization. You've heard the expression "A rising tide raises all boats" (thank you, JFK, for that one). You want to be surrounded by people who are in the same boat with you.

Ron Quintero, a very successful real estate entrepreneur, never graduated from high school. He lived on the streets at times. But he was tenacious and finally got a job with UPS. He wanted more, and he had the curiosity to try something new (again and again) and the ambition to drive him forward. More than that, his wife was right there beside him, sometimes in front of him, keeping him on track. She was just as ambitious for him as he was for himself. She believed in him and helped him believe in himself and aspire for more. Maintaining the right attitude in the people around you is another task. What can you do to help them maintain their positive perspectives?

Curiosity and ambition need to be cultivated. But the right attitude requires even more. The questions I'm asking are, "What is your disposition toward the future, and what kind of mood do you need to maintain to stay on track?" The decisions you make are influenced by your mood. Your leadership is prejudiced by your mood. The job of leadership is emotional (read: mood) and is influenced by your social awareness, relationship management, self-management, and self-awareness. Even if you're not leading a team, you're still leading—yourself. If that's the case, maintaining your mood becomes even more important. And I don't mean just staying positive. Being positive 100 percent of the time is not realistic—it's not even balanced (you simply can't be "up" every minute of every day). Being positive is also not a specific disposition. So what are the specific dispositions that you should maintain to achieve your objectives?

Nurture Creativity

The challenge is to inspire yourself and others around you to sustain the right disposition. Creativity (a creative disposition) is a big part of the answer to that challenge. For many of us, the more creative we feel, the more able we are to face obstacles in our life. When we feel creative, problems no longer look insurmountable. Creativity better equips us to find solutions, and it can positively influence our mood. Creativity is both a source and an outcome of curiosity. Creativity expands ambition. It is seeing new ways of accomplishing things and new things to accomplish.

We need to nurture both our own creativity and the creative instincts or disposition of those around us to succeed. The great thing about it is that creativity is one of those things that feeds on itself; the more creative we are, the more creative we will be. I would go further and say that the more creative we perceive ourselves to be, the more creative we may be. Do you see yourself as creative? Some people may seem to have been born with more than their share of creativity, but creativity is in all our genes. It is born of a host of factors, many of which are in our control. Creativity can be as simple as changing the route you take home from work once in a while. Creativity can be anything from telling a story to your child, to cooking a dish you've never made before, to developing a new marketing strategy, to inventing a new product.

There are myriad ways that we manifest creativity in our lifestyles and in our work. I can almost guarantee that if you are booked solid, then you are creative. You couldn't have achieved what you have without some creativity. It's a matter of consciously identifying your creative acts and harnessing that energy because creativity can be a source of energy and energy is what you need to maintain your curiosity and ambition. Being creative creates its own momentum. Each time you solve a problem or overcome a challenge, think about how energized you feel by your victory. That's the kind of creative energy that perpetuates itself and that will help you stay on track as you innovate in your business.

Learn to recognize the effects of creative energy when you are experiencing it so you can harness that energy for the future. Creativity in and of itself is not enough. It can lead you off track, down blind alleys. It's not just a matter of, "Oh, I'm being creative; let me be." That's the beauty of understanding our own creativity. By identifying how and when we are creative, we can begin to shape our creative force, to direct it where it's needed. Self-management and self-awareness are key. You need to think and behave intentionally about the future.

Scott Berkun, author of *The Myths of Innovation*, says that ideas are combinations of other ideas and creative people are those who come up with more combinations of ideas, find interesting ones faster, and are willing to try them out. He goes on to say that innovation is nothing more than a practice, or a set of habits. That means keeping the "why" of what you're doing, and for the sake of "what," in the forefront of your consciousness and directing energy toward that end. Know where you're going. Create the path that takes you there. Hal Macomber says, "Innovation is a simple act. All it entails is producing something new that others can ask for. Becoming *innovative* requires a commitment to mastery." As a student of business (and life, not to mention other things like Aikido, a martial art from Japan), there are few things more rewarding than pursuing mastery. Innovation is sure to energize you.

But having the willingness to try new things is not enough. You must also be willing to let go of an idea that isn't working. That's the flip side of curiosity. It includes curiosity in our own ideas. Will they work? Are they viable? If not, what's our next idea? I'm not saying you should give up on ideas. I'm saying you should move on from ideas that aren't working. It's not the same thing at all. Moving on is its own form of curiosity. When we are most creative, we are coming up with tons of new ideas at a time. They can't all be good. We will never know what's good and what's not if we don't test them out. Curiosity is the willingness to test our ideas, discard the weakest, and build on the strongest. That's how you will maintain your creative energy.

Maintaining creative energy, staying "up," isn't always easy. Self-defeating thoughts, attitudes, and behaviors can lead to breakdown. We all have a tendency toward creativity. Sadly, that tendency may have been trampled down, starting in childhood, so that we are intimidated by our own creative drives. Remember that Harry Chapin song about the child whose teacher criticized him for drawing trees blue and the sky green, because that's not how it is? Many of us have had childhood experiences just like that, experiences that made us fearful of our own creativity. Our reaction is to undermine our own energy before someone else does—although, beware, that's going to happen, too.

We are susceptible not only to mental or attitudinal self-sabotage, but also to sabotage from immediate external factors (different from the ones that influenced our early development) that can interrupt our balance, throw us off course, or blindside us. Scott Berkun points out that the toughest challenge faced by innovators is how bored the rest of the world is by their ideas, at least at first. It turns out that nothing changes when we're adults—no one really wants us to draw blue trees and green skies, ever. Over the years, I've heard varying statistics about the way our creativity gets killed as we age. Some say that 97 percent of children in kindergarten are creative but that by second grade only 5 percent are. Others say that children in kindergarten use 80 percent of their creative potential on a regular basis and that by the age of 12 the average person is using only 2 percent of his or her creative potential. Suffice to say that in general people aren't getting more creative as they grow up. What happens? Grades happen. The need to have the approval of others happens. This would be terrible news, except that the disease is reversible! The practice of creativity produces more creativity. The practice of innovation produces more innovativeness.

Having the emotional endurance to withstand the early period of any innovation process is the difference between whether a big, new idea survives or withers. Remind yourself that when others are negative or reject your idea, they are often just demonstrating their own aversion to change. We humans are fearful of the new. It's in our nature. Like the ancient fable of the scorpion and the frog—the scorpion just had to sting the frog in the end—it was in the scorpion's nature, even though it meant they both drowned as the frog was carrying the scorpion to the other side of the river.

Self-sabotage and other people's censure is not all you face. There are market factors, too, that can sabotage our creativity: unexpected competitors who might appear on the horizon, new technologies that might render your service obsolete, or changes in consumer tastes. Suddenly your great idea—isn't.

With all these potential sources of breakdown (self, others, and the market), what do you need to support your continued growth, improvement, creativity, and innovation? Do you need external systems, like mastermind groups, a coach, or continuing education? Do you need to take art or dance classes to feel creative and open-minded?

Exercise 1

List the things you have done in the past week, the past month, or the past three months that made you feel creative or that you or others would call creative.

Exercise 2

How creative do you want to be? What are some activities you'd like to do or experiences you'd like to have that would make you feel creative in business and in your personal life?

Exercise 3

Identify in advance what external factors might cause a breakdown and stifle your creativity.

What do *you* need to avoid breakdown and to sustain your mood when breakdown does occur?

Here's a short list of questions that I review periodically when working *on* my business and *on myself* (which, I hope, is a constant). If I get the answers wrong, I'm sure to run into breakdown. By the way, the right answers are obvious:

- Do you ever change your ideas?
- Do you listen, really listen, to people who disagree with you? (You might learn something.)
- Have you changed any of your own treasured opinions or assumptions about the world lately? Have you ever imagined

what the world might be like if it were the exact opposite of
how you think it is?

- Do you tend to try to help people find solutions to obstacles
  they are facing, or do you prefer to criticize?
- Do you stand by the ideas you believe in, even if other people
  think they are silly? Are you threatened by a problem you can't
  solve right away?

A lot less is sacred and more is changeable than you think. As you
develop a practice of creativity, you will be surprised (and delighted)
by the doors it will open in your business and in your life. Go into
the next chapter, and all the chapters that follow, with a big sense of
curiosity and a willingness and a desire to be creative in how you
view your business and its potential. That's the attitude you need to
go beyond booked solid.

4 | Business—Building Blocks

The problem is never how to get new, innovative thoughts into your mind, but how to get old ones out. Every mind is a building filled with archaic furniture. Clean out a corner of your mind and creativity will instantly fill it.

—**Dee Hock**

Whether you want to maintain the current size of your business but would like to change the scope of your responsibilities or you plan to add multiple streams of revenue, find sources of passive revenue, add service providers, deliver your services in a group format, produce products, or create franchising and licensing opportunities, I hope to help you choose the structure that best ensures your professional, financial, and hopefully personal success.

Maybe you are happy with the structure you have in place and simply want to extend it, to make it work better for you. We can do that, too, but bear in mind that even if what we do is as simple as raising prices and seeing fewer clients, there will probably be some new business structuring involved to truly divest the busywork. The architecture of your business is the structures, systems, practices, and relationships of how you do business. It is the structure that enables you to fulfill your commitments. As Fernando Flores, a philosopher, former Chilean politician, and entrepreneur, says, "The work of an organization is making and keeping commitments." Something in the structure of your business will most likely have to change if you truly want to go beyond booked solid. So let's look at the fundamentals of any architecture.

A business building block describes a company's business. Most important, it is the mechanism by which a business generates revenue, which is, after all, the foundation of business. If we're on the same page, our goal is to use these business building blocks to create a business architecture that allows you to make the most money, incur the fewest costs, and expend the least amount of effort. This is easier said than done. Those of us who dedicate our professional lives to serving others often assume that in order to do so, we have to work really hard, all the time. Worse still, we think that if our work doesn't consume our lives, then we're irresponsible or, dare I say, lazy. I know. I've been addicted to the feeling of being busy. I have typically felt most relevant if I work until exhaustion. I have been known to wear my work ethic and my hours logged on my sleeve as a badge of honor. It's neither productive nor healthy to do so. We're looking to feel useful and we think that being busy fills that need, but it's a poor substitute for being effective and truly purposeful.

Right now you may have no idea how you can viably expand your business. Or you may be running an expanding business, but it is not yet fully leveraged. In either case, you have work to do. But it's the kind of work that can take you through what Seth Godin calls "the dip" in his book of the same name: "It's the grueling ten-mile marker in the marathon when the finish line is too far to see. It's when Google had to tough it out with big competitors before becoming #1. It's when your new business has a hundred bills to pay and no clients. In other words, the dip is the long, difficult stretch between starting something and mastering it."

Together we will identify and extend what you have or build a whole new viable business architecture that will get you through the dip. We'll use the following four criteria to measure the success of your new or extended architecture. Keep these in the front of your mind as we work through the rest of the book:

1. *Profitability:* It is highly profitable, with significant margins for the labor associated with it.
2. *Scalability:* Many, if not all, of the areas of your business can be run by employees or independent contractors, who can easily be added as demand dictates.
3. *Excellence:* It allows you to work only in the areas of your greatest strengths, on what energizes you, which, in turn, enables you to be the *best* in your market.

I'm going to take a small side trip here into the topic of what *best* really means. As Seth Godin points out, *best* is a subjective term, ultimately determined by your clients. You can be the *best* fitness trainer in Chicago, the best life coach in Atlanta, or the best marketing consultant in Fargo, at the same time that someone else is the best fitness trainer, life coach, or marketing consultant somewhere else. They don't even have to be somewhere else. So long as your clients think you are the "best" for them—in that place, at that time, for the cost—then you are the best. But—there's always a "but" with things like this—you can only be the best at something at which you excel. You need to have enough talent so that the people who share your worldview will think you're the best. If you never went past high-school orchestra, you probably can't be the best cellist in the world. Enough said. Onward to criteria 4:

4. *Leverage:* It can expand without demanding much more time from you. As it grows, you can, if you choose to, work less and earn more.

Okay—now that we've established the right assessment criteria, we can move to the next step. What are the choices? I'd like to make choosing the structural building blocks for your new business model easy. That's probably not possible. It's a hard process. Whoever said that nothing good comes easy could very well have been referring to redesigning the architecture of your business. Yet, often we think that to make a change is too complicated. What's really happening is that we are the complication. We are making something more difficult than it needs to be. There are all sorts of reasons why this might happen. It could be because we don't understand well enough what we need to do. Other times making things more complicated than they need to be is a technique of giving ourselves a way out by sabotaging our own future. Don't do that. I'll attempt to simplify our work, if you'll think simply about it. Agreed?

We'll start by looking at the nine most common types of building blocks in the service business. Along the way, I'll give you examples of how other service professionals have used these different building blocks to go beyond booked solid. My goal is to start by whetting your appetite for growth and then to fill you up with substantive information on the options available.

There is no one-size-fits-all way of doing this. There are certain types of business building blocks that are common across the different service industries and that have been used successfully to create businesses that meet the four criteria I mentioned earlier: profitability, scalability, excellence, and leverage. Inside each business, the architecture is relatively unique.

Even if you think that you already have the architecture you want, don't skip this part. It's always good to review the options again, if only to confirm that you have built the right structure. There's a good chance, too, that you are not fully conscious of all the elements of your business architecture. You may have business building blocks in your business that you aren't even aware of. You can't extend the architecture you have until you are fully aware of what you have.

It's like putting an addition on a house. You can't tear down a wall and start building out if you don't know first what's inside the wall—something structural, ducts or pipes, or other obstacles—and other important information.

As you read on, keep this top-of-mind: When you design a new business architecture, you may in fact be creating a new business. Any experienced business leader or entrepreneur will tell you it's essential to know what business you're in. If you're a chiropractor who is currently working with patients and you decide that you want to open locations all over the country, you'll be going into a new business—the business of operations and management or perhaps even the real estate business.

It is also important to keep in mind that different building blocks can be combined. In fact, this is most often the case. No two business architectures are exactly alike, and no architecture is built purely from one building block. As you will see in the case studies in Chapter 14, some of the most successful entrepreneurs have used aspects of two or more different business building blocks to design the architecture of their companies.

Common Business Building Blocks

Let's now review the nine building blocks that may be part of your business architecture. Remember, not all of the business blocks are part of every business.

Franchising

According to the *Financial Times,* if sales by U.S. franchise businesses were translated into gross national product (GNP), they would qualify as the seventh-largest economy in the world. Clearly, *franchising* is a proven concept. Hold on, though. Franchising is not easy to succeed at, and it won't work for everyone. You'll need research to determine whether franchising is right for your business.

Franchising is a way to quickly expand your business into new markets by partnering with businesspeople who want to buy a business-in-a-box. The franchisor sells one or more franchises to professionals who deliver the service and products in a defined geographical area and/or to a specific market segment under the company's brand, using the company's infrastructure, resources, experience, and marketing. The franchisee invests an initial fee along with start-up costs and pays the franchisor an ongoing percentage of the profits. Some franchisors also charge annual fees on top of this percentage. The business is appealing to franchisees because the business structure and systems are already developed, so it's a quick-start opportunity. Because franchise businesses are developed to deliver consistency, the customer knows what to expect each and every time. The challenge for the franchisor is to partner with franchisees that are able to maintain a standard quality of service. With each new partner, the franchisor increases the leverage they are getting out of their original business—more money, less work.

Brandon Hartsell is using franchising to build his string of Sunstone Yoga studios in Dallas, Texas. Once Brandon was booked solid as a yoga teacher at his original studio, he created a teacher-training program to develop more teachers for his one studio. Once all of his new teachers were booked solid, he opened several more studios on his own, using teachers from his own training program. And just as Brandon had planned, Sunstone Yoga kept growing. So Brandon implemented the next stage of his plan and began offering a franchise program in which qualified applicants, from the pool of certified Sunstone teachers, could apply to buy their own franchise of a Sunstone Yoga studio. Because he and his partner had been meticulous about documenting their processes and systems from the beginning and because they knew that teaching standards were maintained through their certification program, they were able to ensure the quality of the Sunstone franchise studios without making further investments of time or money.

Brian Scudamore, CEO and founder of 1-800-Got-Junk?, got into the junk business at age 19. With $700 down, he bought a beat-up old truck so he could make some extra cash by hauling away unwanted junk. Two years later, he turned it into a full-time operation; and now he's franchised his junk removal business, differentiating himself by establishing a reputation (carried through by his franchisees) of providing clean trucks and clean drivers, up-front fees, and on-time service. Franchisees join in the marketing, finding strategic places to park their perpetually clean and shiny white-and-blue trucks, even wearing big blue wigs and holding up 1-800-Got-Junk? signs and waving wildly at passing traffic (a marketing tactic outlined in their franchise package). It hardly sounds like the junk business, and it has annual revenues of around $100 million.

Licensing

The *licensing* business building block shares some similarities with the franchise business building block, but it's different in a few ways. The greatest difference is that the relationship between the licensee and the licensor is not as close as the relationship between franchisors and franchisees, and the licensee generally has much more freedom. The license adds revenue to the licensor's business, but the licensees may use their own brands and set their own marketing strategy, hours, and business plan. The licensee is purchasing the right to use specific intellectual property, like content, software, or some proprietary protocol.

Like a franchise, an intellectual property license commonly has several component parts, including a term, a territory, and renewal, as well as other limitations specific to what is being licensed. Unlike franchising, licensors can sell to more than one licensee within a territory and do not have control over the licensee's business structure.

Some, but not all, licensing models require that a percentage of all future revenues are passed back to the licensor. Other licensing models require that the licensee pay only an up-front licensing fee for use of the material for a given term. Renewal fees are then required to extend the term.

Training the Trainer

Teaching others how to provide the services you've been providing is another excellent way to bring your work to more people who need it. In order to do this, you either need to have a proprietary way of delivering your services or at least be so exceptionally good at training others to excel in the field you're teaching, training, or coaching that your market will accept no substitute, not even a copycat. Ideally, you have some proprietary protection, like a copyright or a trademark, although it's my experience that in the end there are always people who will try to steal your ideas, which is why it's also helpful to be at the top of your field.

One of the important factors to consider, as it relates to the training-the-trainer building block, is how you will deliver these services. In order to make it scalable, you have to be able to serve increasingly larger numbers of clients. For example, you can deliver your training in a group format and, in turn, certify others to deliver the same training to still more groups. If you plan on developing this building block in a one-room schoolhouse, so to speak, then you better make sure you know how you're going to grow it and take yourself out of the equation as the primary service provider.

What enabled Brandon Hartsell to move beyond booked solid at his first Sunstone Yoga studio? He created a teacher-training program to develop more teachers for his studio so he could offer more classes while still maintaining his rigorous teaching standards and ensuring that anyone teaching at his studio adhered to his protocols and shared his philosophy. From there the next logical step, as you saw earlier, was to franchise the systems and processes of both the teacher-training program and the studios. He created a certification process that ensured the continuing high quality of teachers trained in his method. In turn, as the new teachers were certified and were ready train others, some of them would choose the franchise route so they could open their own Sunstone Yoga studios, which followed Brandon's protocols and philosophy.

Ron Quintero went from sleeping on the street to become the founder of My Resource Center, Mortgage Leaders Edge, Debt Advisory, and Finance This Home. Ron took a slightly different route to incorporating the training-the-trainer building block in his business. He had built up so much real estate experience with his various related businesses in Orange County that he was able to sell off his primary real estate service businesses and dedicate himself to training others to do what he did. Instead of using the training to build his business, training the trainer became his business. Take note of that; I mentioned earlier that there is always a chance when you're building a new business architecture that you'll end up in a new business, just like Ron Quintero did.

Branding

Once you are booked solid, you can open other storefronts, buy out competitors, and start related businesses—in other words, build on the brand that you have created. Richard Branson is one of the highest-profile examples of building on a brand name. The Virgin brand started as an independent record label, and now it's on everything from airplanes to wedding dresses. See this diversification as a case of an ultrasuccessful idiosyncratic founder and CEO doing whatever he wants. In your case, if you have a location where you offer your services, you might add locations, or you might add events, if that's what you offer. Whatever you sell, you can offer more opportunities for others to buy it through different channels, in different venues, and in different forms, all under the banner of your brand name. The best part is that you can hire others to deliver the services based on your methods and protocols. To work best, your brand needs to be well known to your target market and other professionals in your industry, be a trusted source for what you offer, and be known as the crème de la crème, associated with the highest quality.

Dr. Mike Berkley's name on an acupuncturist's fertility practice is enough to quadruple the number of patients. Dr. Berkley, an acupuncturist, is able to approach other practicing acupuncturists, offer to acquire and/or rebrand their businesses as the Berkley Center for Reproductive Wellness and Women's Health, and even take 50 percent of the earnings. Why? Because of the Berkley brand name that he's built up over the years. How? Early on he decided to focus on a niche market. Since 1996, he has marketed himself exclusively to the community of couples dealing with fertility issues, and his practice has grown accordingly. His is one of only five practices in the country that focuses exclusively on treating infertility with acupuncture and herbal medicine. When he started, he was the only one. It was a golden branding opportunity, and he took it.

On a smaller scale (stay tuned because the future is bright), Lori Kliman and Heather White, founders of Cupcakes by Heather and Lori, a bakery that sells cupcakes and other baked goods in Vancouver, British Columbia, have built a brand name in their city by attending community events, giving away product, and supplying cupcakes to coffee shops and grocery stores. Now that their local brand is strong, they plan to offer franchising opportunities—adding another building block in their business architecture.

Intellectual Property

The *intellectual property* business building block is based on taking a typical service and turning it into a slate of information products and programs that can be widely distributed and easily consumed by the customer. I can use myself as the example here. I took a typical service—marketing consulting—and turned it into a scalable business by converting the services I offered into systems and protocols that can be understood and implemented through books, CDs, workshops, keynote speeches, and distance learning courses, many of which are delivered by other professionals I've trained and certified. It leveraged my skills more effectively so I could go beyond working with one client at a time. This building block is often a natural combination with licensing if others, under their own names, can use what you've created.

Jonathan Hunt, founder and CEO of FundNet.ca, never planned on getting into the intellectual property business. It just happened. First, he was a financial planner, then he saw an opportunity on the Internet well before anyone else did. He created an online financial planning tool with proprietary software for his clients. Then one day, another financial planner asked him how much he'd sell his system for. She not only bought his system, she also invited Jonathan to speak at her company's chairman's appreciation council meeting. More buyers materialized, and Jonathan added the intellectual property building block to his business architecture. Now you might even say he's in the software business.

Full-Service

The *full-service* business building block takes a one-person operation that offers one primary service and turns it into a full-service firm—a one-stop shop for all your clients' needs. A fitness trainer can create a center offering a slate of health and wellness services. A virtual assistant could create a firm that handles all administrative, marketing, and business operation needs by bringing in other contractors to execute the additional services. Remember—make sure that the additional services you offer meet the current needs of your clients. The services ought to be services that the clients are already buying. You can't create a need for clients; but if they already use the types of services you plan to offer, they may consider bringing their business to you. After all, they already trust you.

Some business transactions depend on a number of services to meet all of the customers needs and are perfect candidates for the full-service approach. For example, to purchase a house, the customer needs a realtor, a mortgage broker, a title officer, an appraiser, and a home inspector. Instead of sending the customer to outside service professionals, you can create a full-service business or one-stop shopping enterprise so the customer can do all transactions in-house and you can make a profit on each part of the sale.

That's what Ron Quintero did in Orange County. After owning a number of related real estate businesses—escrow company, mortgage company, real estate licensing school, property management company, home owners' insurance company, and appraisal firm—Ron Quintero created a boutique firm that was a total-solution provider. It sold homes and provided the financing and everything else you might need when you're buying real estate. Ultimately, as you saw earlier, he was so successful in his niche that he was able to sell the related businesses and the boutique firm and focus instead on training others to do what he did.

In a totally different industry, Dr. Mike Berkley used the full-service business building block to create the Berkley Center for Reproductive Wellness and Women's Health, a chain of wellness centers that specialize in treating male and female infertility using acupuncture, herbal medicine, yoga, meditation, nutrition, and other modalities. Dr. Berkley, an acupuncturist, saw there was an opportunity in offering services delivered by other trained practitioners. By providing a one-stop wellness center, Dr. Berkley has made himself and his centers one of the leading "go to" resources for fertility issues in the country.

Network Marketing

The *network marketing* business building block is a combination of direct marketing and franchising. You might hear it referred to as direct marketing or multilevel marketing. It describes an enterprise that recruits salespeople, who in turn recruit their own salespeople, and so on, creating a network or multilevel marketing business structure. You might see the salespeople labeled anything from distributors, to independent business owners (IBOs), to franchise owners, sales consultants, beauty consultants, or some other creative moniker. At each level, the salespeople earn commissions for selling a product or a service and earn additional sales commissions from their downline recruits. Like franchising, royalties are paid from the sales of individual franchise operations to the franchisor and to an area or region manager, except that in some network marketing programs there can be seven or more levels of people receiving royalties from one downstream person's sales.

Thinking that this sounds familiar, and not in a good way? Network marketing has an image problem. It is often difficult to distinguish legitimate network marketing from illegal pyramid schemes. A recent example is Burnlounge.com (a site that set up a multilevel system for buying and selling music and movies), which the Federal Trade Commission (FTC) considered a pyramid scheme. Although the FTC allowed Burnlounge.com to stay in business, it was forced to discontinue the network marketing portion of its business model. Even when a network marketing business is legitimate in its business practices, it may sell products that seem questionable at best, like oils to grow your hair, massage cream to melt away fat, or juice that cures fatal diseases. If you can combine a real, relevant product or service offering with a network marketing business model, like SendOutCards.com has done or others (Arbonne health and beauty products is another example), then you might just build something remarkable.

Kody Batemen founded SendOutCards.com to help people become what he calls "card senders." That's the kind of person you always wanted to be but never get around to being—someone who remembers everyone's birthday and sends them a card on time, someone who sends thank you cards to friends and business colleagues, someone who has organized tickler systems that support their business marketing efforts, and so on. Bateman has developed technology that enables people to send cards out from their desktop. We're talking about real, physical cards, the kind made from old-fashioned paper and delivered via snail mail, the kind you can put on your desk or mantle to remind you that the person who sent the card was thinking of you. But it's all done from your computer. No trying to find time to get to the card store, no hunting for your friend or work colleague's address for the umpteenth time, no going to the post office because you don't have stamps, no trying to remember to get the envelope in the mailbox. SendOutCards.com even has technology that enables you to create your own handwriting font so your cards look like they were written by hand. How cool is that? And Bateman has structured the company using the network marketing business building block. It's worked wonderfully for Kody Batemen because of the enthusiasm of SendOutCards.com users. They want to pass the word along. So why not make money while they're at it by signing new people up?

Social Networking

Online social networking sites, like LinkedIn.com, flickr.com, friendster.com, and myspace.com have become the virtual business structure flavor of the month. You can also add membership sites and organizations to this category. Great as they are, the structure is hardly new. Social networking businesses have existed off-line in bricks-and-mortar, flesh-and-blood reality for ages. If you belong to a professional association, you've probably noticed that it employs social networking. Business leads and networking groups like Business Network International (BNI) use social networking. I love the *social networking* business building block because it's based on the natural human desire to connect with and collaborate with others.

Lori and Heather, think tasty cupcakes, belong to an organization of women entrepreneurs through which they can vet their new ideas and see what works for other businesses and cross-appropriate. Mike Berkley relied, at least at first, on referrals from his network of colleagues. Strategic alliances are frequently another form of social networking. Ron Quintero estimates that 40 percent of his marketing initiatives are based on joint ventures. He drives business to his partners, and they in turn drive business to him.

Not everyone loves social networks. Sometimes it can be difficult to get businesspeople to talk openly with each other, online or in person. Some people like to keep their contacts for themselves or hold their ideas close to the chest. Ultimately, though, you will benefit more from sharing than you will from hoarding.

One thing to bear in mind—a good social network is made of lots of small, networked groups. According to anthropologist Robin Dunbar, group sizes larger than 150 generally require more restricted rules, laws, enforced policies, and regulations to maintain a stable cohesion, so they are less apt for social networking purposes. This is what Dunbar calls the Rule of 150. If you're thinking about adopting the social networking business building block, you will need to consider how to create groups of less then 150 people who are still interconnected.

The Better Mousetrap

Ralph Waldo Emerson said, "Build a better mousetrap, and the world will beat a path to your door." In this case, Emerson was not quite right. Legions of innovators have seen their "better mousetraps" fall by the wayside because the public just wasn't interested. Remember Kozmo.com, the online convenience store that offered people in big cities a way to get a pint of ice cream and a new toothbrush delivered to their door any time, night or day? Maybe you don't. See my point? Unfortunately, it turned out that while the idea seemed innovative, people were not, in fact, willing to pay the necessary premium for their instant toothbrush.

The *better mousetrap* business building block describes a business structure that offers a superior or innovative way of delivering services that people want and are willing to pay for, if necessary. FreshDirect.com is a great example. It turns out people do want groceries delivered to their door, but during normal waking hours. Think of eBay.com versus traditional auction houses. Remember trekking to the library and sneezing your way through the stacks to do research? Well, now you just do a Google search. How about Amazon.com? With its gigantic inventory and preference tracking technology, the convenience of shopping online and getting on-target suggestions of books you might like trumps the shipping costs you could save by going to a traditional brick-and-mortar bookstore.

The value of a better mousetrap is assessed by the needs of the market. As Hal Macomber says, "There is nothing of value independent of a person saying it is valued." If you can deliver the services (or product) your potential clients really want, in an innovative way, that's also easy to market, you might just build something remarkable. Jonathan Hunt did it with FundNet.ca. The reason people wanted to buy his intellectual property was because he had built something unique with his online financial planning tool and client software. No one had thought to do it in quite the way he did before, and once he'd done it, there was no point in reinventing the wheel. Jonathan Hunt built a better mousetrap, and the world has been beating a path to his door, or at least knocking. In Jonathan's case, Emerson was right.

Mike Berkley's idea for a fertility center offering not just acupuncture but also related health and wellness services was a better mousetrap. So was Brian Scudamore's idea of creating a junk removal business known for cleanliness, timeliness, and friendliness; it almost sounds like an oxymoron. In fact, it was just a better mousetrap.

Design What's Constructible

One last word: Just because you choose a business structure that *should* work for you, does not mean it *will* work for you. In other words, just because you can, for example, license the intellectual property in your business does not mean that licensing will be successful for you. Unless you are a leader in your particular business niche (remember the excellence criteria), licensing may not be viable. Once you've chosen a general direction and the building blocks that you think are appropriate, you need to delve further in your research. Devour resources on the different building blocks you are considering to familiarize yourself with the depth and the nuance possible with each structure. Keep in mind the strategies and the criteria as you think about what might work for you. Don't decide on a design and then evaluate its constructability; design what's constructible.

Designing a new or extended business architecture is a big undertaking. I've tried to keep this simple. I know it can be mind-bending at times to reconceive your business. We've been looking at *how* to build your bigger, better business with the building blocks available to you. Before we jump into designing the particular structure that's right for you, we need to lay some more foundation. As I said at the beginning, this book is the *how* and the *why* of making the leap, of going beyond booked solid. Even if you understand all the practical, tangible actions I've suggested so far (the *how*), you may not succeed. To be truly successful, you need to be fully prepared for the future—and that means mentally, as well as practically. We've already talked about your attitude and how to cultivate ambition, curiosity, and creativity so you can innovate in your business. Let's look again at this mental preparation from a new angle—the *why* of why some people succeed (and others don't).

5 | How Can You Get There?— Preparing Yourself for the Future

Prediction is very difficult, especially about the future.
—Niels Bohr

You are ambitious and filled with curiosity. You have harnessed your creative energy to the service of your goals. You are open to the future. You've even begun to explore the building blocks you will use in the design of your new business architecture. Brilliant! But there's another important factor in your mental preparation that we haven't yet discussed. We cannot just be an advocate for our future. We need to inquire about the future. We need to be reflective, to listen to the world. After all, what is our curiosity and creativity for? It is to learn new things. Yes, to learn. Think of how much you may have learned so far in this book. Just because we've looked at some business building blocks doesn't mean that the learning is done and it's time to be "doing." There's no "time to learn" and "time to do." We are always learning (if we're growing and our business is growing). We are always doing. That's working *on yourself*, while working *in* and *on* your business.

But how do we learn? We can come to the threshold of learning new things from different directions. I'm going to suggest one that I think is the most effective. Approach new things (everything new is a learning experience) with openness and with full knowledge of your own assets and limitations as a *discloser.*

Who or what is a discloser? Everyone is. You are. I am. Does it mean I have to pour my heart out to everyone? Disclose my deepest secrets to my business colleagues? No. Don't worry. Let me explain.

Be a Conscious Discloser

Using language that is often impenetrable by even the brightest of thinkers, Charles Spinosa, Fernando Flores, and Hubert L. Dreyfus in *Disclosing New Worlds: Entrepreneurship, Democratic Action, and the Cultivation of Solidarity,* suggest that "massive changes in style generally occur when there is cross-appropriation among subworlds." Huh? Yes, that's the first thing I said, too. But it's an incredibly important concept and not actually as tricky as it sounds, so hang in there. For our purposes, *cross-appropriation* just means taking an idea from one area (a subworld) and using it in another area. *Gee, this mill wheel really grinds up the wheat but, boy, it rolls nicely, too. Maybe there's an idea here for a two-wheeled machine I could ride into town on.* Wheel-shaped things existed for a long time before anyone thought to cross-appropriate them for bicycles.

Cross-appropriation requires that we overcome historical attitudes or ideas, that we understand that what we think of as paradigms (as "givens") are most often our own creation and much more fluid than we imagined. It is about questioning our beliefs of how it is and how it should be. Instead, we should ask, "What is possible?"

According to Spinosa, Flores, and Dreyfus, "Cross-appropriation takes place when one disclosive space takes over from another disclosive space a practice that it could not generate on its own but that it finds useful." See what I mean about impenetrable language? Before you start lamenting, "What on earth is a disclosive space?" know that we all have our own disclosive space. Essentially it means the way each one of us sees the world as we operate in that world. It is our personal perspective, only more. It is our way of understanding how complex structures are interrelated and fit together. Children can rarely understand things outside their disclosive space. But as we mature and our thinking becomes more sophisticated, we begin to see things outside our disclosive space, to understand things outside our own direct experience.

Yet, even adults can have very narrow disclosive spaces. Here's another way of thinking of it. We are all disclosers, operating in our individual disclosive spaces; we are people operating from our unique perspectives. It's the reason why two people can witness the same thing in the same place at the same time and see two different events unfold. I'm sure you've heard the stories about witnesses at trials who describe something as simple as a car accident in vastly different ways. Think about arguments you've had with your lover or spouse or someone else close to you. And you just can't understand why they don't see things your way or why they seem to deliberately misremember what you said yesterday. It's because each person has different distinctions, different perspectives, and different points of reference. It's why Akira Kurosawa's film *Rashomon,* which tells the story of a man's murder from the perspective of all the different characters, each of whom has a completely different view of what happened, is so brilliant that it is considered a classic and is often imitated.

The actions we take reflect our way of seeing and being in the world. When people give different reports of the same incident, we often think that they are lying or not paying attention. Neither explains the phenomenon completely. As Hal puts it, "Our intentions and commitments brighten aspects of the world," like when you decide to buy a new car and suddenly the make of car you're considering buying is everywhere on the road, though you'd never noticed that make before; likewise, say you decide to franchise, and suddenly you notice different franchise businesses everywhere.

Our disclosive space changes, too. Our mood, for example, has an enormous effect on what we are able to "see" in the world. I'm sure you've experienced how a bad mood can get in the way of your noticing the wonderful world around you. Fortunately, the opposite holds true, too. A good mood can lift you up through the less-than-good times. High spirits can help you face challenges. Once we are conscious of ourselves as disclosers, as people who each exist in our unique disclosive spaces, then we can begin to see and act with better intentionality. Knowing and understanding the limits of our world-view will automatically begin to open us up to new ways of seeing things, new ways of being. It will enable us to see things as others see them (sometimes). In designing a new architecture for your business, you need to be able to understand and to move outside your current disclosive space. What's inside you will affect how well you will execute the strategies and the techniques in this book.

Do you want to go beyond booked solid? Then recognize yourself as a discloser. Everyone is a discloser, whether they know it or not. The important thing is to develop an awareness of your discloser qualities, to become a *conscious* discloser. You'll notice this theme of identifying qualities you already possess recurring throughout the book—creativity, curiosity, discloser, and so on. Sure, you may be a discloser already, but you need to know it. What's the big deal?, you may be thinking. If I'm already a discloser (or ambitious, or creative), why do I need to read this? *Because we can't fully benefit from what we have until we are conscious of it.* We already know we need to be conscious of our weaknesses—to steer clear of them. We forget that we need to be conscious of our strengths, too—to allow them to fuel us. Only by being tuned in to our strengths can we truly exploit them.

This is all a fancy way of saying that you need to be open to learning and incorporating new ideas, new methods, new systems, and new experiences. And I'm making it one level fancier by offering you a term to use—conscious discloser. *A conscious discloser is someone who can see, understand, and adopt things from outside his or her disclosive space.* Okay, so it's not so fancy after all.

Being a conscious discloser is not just about how you learn; it is also about how you apply that learning. After all, a person could read 10 books a week on a variety of topics outside her disclosive space; but if she never applies any of what she gleans from the books, then so what. Being a know-it-all is not the same thing as being a conscious discloser, nor is being a critic—"Oh, I know that already; my way is better." In the end it is what you do with what you learn that matters, and this is where productive disclosers excel. They are people who learn and apply constantly. And their goals are more important then their current way of doing or seeing things. You need to be a conscious discloser to build a bigger, better business.

Be Ahistorical

Because being a conscious discloser is so important, I'm going to come at the definition again from another angle offered by Spinosa, Flores, and Dreyfus: *A conscious discloser is someone who can be ahistorical.* People who are ahistorical are *not* prisoners of their past. When we are not prisoners of our past, then we can change our future, regardless of our history. In a way, it's how people think about the classic American dream—a person who comes from an unlikely background making it big. That might be ahistorical. The alternative is to be constantly and utterly shaped by your past without relief—to be, in a sense, a victim of your past. My father did such and such; therefore, I'll do such and such because it's all I know. Not that there is necessarily anything wrong with following in your family's footsteps, but do it intentionally, not by default. You can't escape your past, and you will inevitably be shaped by your past, but you are in control of whether your past is forcing you down a certain path or whether you have chosen it. To be ahistorical is a way of approaching the world. It describes how you *are* in the world, your way of being.

Apolo Anton Ohno is a two-time Olympic Gold medal winner for short-track speed skating. Apolo reached the pinnacle of a sport based on tucking yourself into the smallest, most aerodynamic ball and skating as fast as possible around an oval. Now that takes a certain kind of focus inside a very specific disclosive space. So, it was all the more amazing when Apolo competed in an entirely different field on the TV show *Dancing with the Stars* and won. When he was asked after the competition what he'd learned, other than how to do the paso doble, jive, and samba, he said, "I've seen a whole new way of being." Wow! Now that's someone who is open to new things.

The rebellious son, for example, is not ahistorical. Rebellion is essentially acting out in the present against the past. The rebellious son doesn't appreciate himself or his future. Rather his future is an expression of the loathing he has for his past. He is not a conscious discloser. Imagine, by contrast, a farmer's daughter who goes off to study advertising at a big university in the city. She meets a city doctor, falls in love, and convinces him to come back and live on the farm with her. Back on the farm, the daughter reconfigures the operations of the farm, cross-appropriating practices and concepts she learned while she was away. She is ahistorical, shaped by her past, but not imprisoned by her past. She chooses to come back to the farm, but she brings with her new ideas from other disclosive spaces. She is ahistorical. She might just as well have stayed in the city with her doctor husband, so long as her decision was a choice for a different future and not a choice against her past. We can all be ahistorical. It's a matter of creating new history that is not governed by our past.

To make history, we need to escape the confines of history. Conscious disclosers are the history makers. So what exactly is it that history makers do that is ahistorical?

- *They articulate.* They give language to something that hasn't been said before. Naming something is an innovation in itself. Luke Howard, a British Quaker in the nineteenth century, was the first person to name the cloud types—cumulus, stratus, and cirrus. Articulation is innovation, and it is the necessary precursor to further innovation. Our farmer's daughter articulated her desire to return to the farm on her own terms. Because she did, the doctor followed her there. Jeff Bezos, the founder of Amazon.com, articulated the idea of an online bookstore. Venture capitalists offered him money to create it.
- *They reconfigure.* They take what they already have and do something different and new with it. The farmer's daughter was a master reconfigurer. Bezos reconfigured the concept of a bricks-and-mortar bookstore into a virtual bookstore to serve his, and his new customer's, needs and desires.
- *They cross-appropriate.* They take ideas, concepts, mechanisms, models, and so on from one industry/society/community/ or other source outside their disclosive space and use the new ideas to create a new world for themselves. It wasn't the same old farm when the daughter got done with it. And it certainly wasn't the same old bookstore (or Internet, for that matter) when Bezos got done. Actually, Bezos isn't done yet. Amazon.com keeps creating new "subworlds."

Being a conscious discloser and understanding its implications will help you to act more intentionally—to open up bigger and bigger spaces (subworlds). Intentionality is one of the hallmarks of success. Brandon Hartsell knew exactly where he wanted to go with Sunstone

Yoga from the beginning, and he knew how he wanted to get there. Even when he was teaching at his first small studio, he had a vision of the teacher-training program he would develop and the franchised studios he would grow into. Where do you want to go? And how do you intend to get there?

Exercise 1

Articulate your objectives. Be as specific as you can, but write down everything, even if it seems vague. Put your objectives on a time line:

In one year, I want my business to _____.

In three years, I'd like to achieve _____ in my personal life.

You will find that the very process of writing down and articulating your dreams will open up new ideas.

Exercise 2

Make a list of what you will need to reconfigure in your life or business to achieve your objectives.

Exercise 3

Make a list of what you can cross-appropriate to better serve your objectives and reconfiguration. Start by thinking of good ideas you think other people have. Then see how or if those ideas might be put to use for your own ends.

Learning Methods

Now that you know what a discloser is and (surprise, surprise!) that you are one (I know you are, but what am I? Saying that was irresistible), you understand better how you learn and apply what you learn—as a discloser, of course. In order to go beyond booked solid, there's a lot to learn. There are many theories about how we learn things, most of which are, in my opinion, just a lot of . . .

Yes, we each have affinities for certain learning styles. But if we don't have a range of learning styles, then we'll never be someone who learns well. "I can't learn that way. Show me a different way." In the end, those can be excuses. It's okay not to figure things out. We can't figure everything out all the time. But we still need to try, no matter what the style. After all, how we learn is just another disclosive space. A conscious discloser is someone who can learn in different environments.

Yet, despite all the theories on learning, fundamentally, we all learn in the same basic way. Virtually all of what we learn in the world is through copying. We learn from seeing how others do something or think about something, and then we imitate them. To learn new things, we need to consciously place ourselves in circumstances where there is an opportunity to learn how others think and how they act. We need to be constant observers (of others and ourselves) to accelerate our learning.

The Training Within Industry (TWI) learning method is one of the best examples of the point I'm making. TWI was developed during World War II to train the flood of women who would be entering the workforce when the men went off to war (think Rosie the Riveter). It was a teaching method that provided rapid and constant training based on three related programs: developing (1) skill in instruction, (2) skill in work methods, and (3) skill in leading other people. The program was presented in four steps: preparation, presentation, application, and testing. The method was so successful that it was introduced in Japan during postwar rebuilding efforts. The basic framework of TWI exists in Toyota Motor Corporation's lean manufacturing model to this day (by the way, *lean* means most efficient, least wasteful). The company's manufacturing model is seen as foundational to Toyota's phenomenal success in continuous improvement and, more importantly, in its ability to sustain those improvements. At Toyota, job instruction is described in five parts:

1. Identify the important steps in the process (this could be any business or manufacturing process).
2. For each important step, identify the key issues to pay attention to.
3. Clarify why it's a key issue.
4. Apply what you've learned.
5. Test, if possible, to demonstrate competence.

At the beginning of World War II, the first job the new American workforce needed to tackle was making lenses (for use in industrial processes and for industrial products, as well as for things like gun sights). Typically, teaching people how to make lenses took five years. Using the TWI approach, that time was reduced to five months. Impressive results! After a few years, they went back to see if they could shorten the process. This time they got it down to five days. How do you like them apples? Oh, I know what you may be thinking. But no, there weren't any significant changes in technology. They just taught the workers differently—simplified the learning process. Simplified the teaching process. Do both for the purpose of the pursuit of mastery. In the process, you'll discover an entirely new way of being.

When in doubt, think of Apolo Anton Ohno. And while you likely have no plans to compete on *Dancing with the Stars* anytime soon, it is that kind of openness to learning new things, learning a whole new way of being, that you need to have to successfully build a bigger, better business. And if you need to wind down at night after a challenging day, learning the paso doble could be a great way to relieve stress and take your mind off business worries at the same time.

6 | The Right Architecture for You—and Keeping It Flexible

The bend in the road is not the end of the road unless you refuse to take the turn.

—Anonymous

Overwhelmed? If you've come this far, you've done a lot of work already, whether you know it or not. Being mentally prepared can go a long way toward managing that out-of-control feeling you might get every time you think about redesigning your business and the work to be done. Let's put that mental preparation to work. It's time to get back to *how* you'll build your bigger, better business. You might be thinking, "How do I choose the right business building blocks?" Or maybe you're thinking, "I want to do everything—licensing, franchising, training the trainer, building a better mousetrap, the works." Well, you can't. You need to choose or, better yet, develop a clear set of options.

51

The Problem of Choice

Speaking of choosing . . . have you noticed how difficult making choices seems to be when you have too many options? It's easy to assume that the more choices you have the better you'll feel about making a choice, but that may not be the case. Herbert Simon, the 1978 Nobel Laureate in Economics, said that any business that tried to make decisions based on how to "maximize" its returns would bankrupt itself in a never-ending search for the best option. Instead, what successful businesses do is attempt to "satisfice," by which Simon meant they are happy with results that are "good enough."

Satisficing is not the same thing as settling. It does not mean accepting something less than perfect (or remarkable) because you don't want to improve. The opposite is, in fact, true. By understanding and working with the idea of satisficing, a business is better able to implement continuous improvements to its structure and operations, to practice continuous learning, what the Japanese call *kaizen*. In fact, the way I see it . . . satisficing is what makes *kaizen* possible. Seeking perfection usually results in indecision. Indecision is the antithesis of improvement. If we become hamstrung trying to achieve perfection, then there will, in the end, never be any improvement. If instead we are able to continue moving forward, then we can constantly improve. "The journey of a thousand miles begins with one step"; or as Bill Murray, the esteemed actor/philosopher, says in the film *What About Bob?*, "Baby steps, baby steps."

We will never accomplish anything if we wait for perfection to start. As Henri-Frédéric Amiel, a nineteenth-century Swiss philosopher, poet, and critic, said, "The man who insists on seeing with perfect clearness before he decides, never decides." This is by no means the same thing as compromising. To compromise is to accept that things cannot be better (or can never be perfect). Waiting for perfection is its own compromise because you are choosing inaction over action (a compromise), choosing indecision over a decision (yes, a compromise). The notion of perfection is inherently a flawed concept. How do we really know what is perfect? We can never know the future 100 percent, so how could we know what will be truly perfect? Actually, if you think about it, a perfectionist is really just a control freak, someone who is constantly trying to manipulate and control outcomes that can't be controlled by one individual. To satisfice is to find a good solution and build on it. How much better does that sound?

It's also been suggested by researchers, including the economist Herbert Simon, that too much choice can be demotivating. In a study by psychologists Daniel Kahneman and Amos Tversky, shoppers who were offered free samples of six different jams were more likely to buy one than shoppers who were offered free samples of 24 types of jams. Students who are offered six topics they can write about for extra credit are more likely to write a paper than students who are offered 30 topics to write about.

Barry Schwartz, a professor of social theory and social action at Swarthmore College and the author of *The Paradox of Choice: Why More Is Less*, suggests that it has to do with the way that we measure opportunity costs. Instead of calculating opportunity cost as the value of the most attractive alternative, we seem to picture an idealistic composite of all the available options. The more options we have, the more idealistic the picture we paint, and, subsequently, the more stressed we become about making a choice. All of this choice leads to a harder time settling on a choice that we think will please us, let alone satisfy us.

I could have offered even more nuanced descriptions of the business building blocks and their possible combinations into new business architectures; but then this book might become less, rather than more, helpful. I've limited your choices to the most fundamental options, so your process of eliminating candidates is easier and choosing the most appropriate model is less stressful—but, of course, that doesn't mean these are the only options available. I suggest that you base your ultimate choice not on what you think is the most ideal or will make you as successful as Oprah, but rather on what will "satisfice." I know it sounds contradictory to say that I want you to choose based on what you believe will be only satisfying rather than ideal, especially coming from the guy to call when you're tired of thinking small; but the research suggests this will help you make a quicker choice with which you will ultimately be satisfied and on which you will build a bigger, better business. One caveat—you have to stick with your choice so that you can make it through the dip I mentioned earlier, that "long, difficult stretch between starting something and mastering it."

As you have likely noticed, almost all of the business building blocks we looked at can be combined with one another. Many of the businesses I mentioned popped up as examples in more than one building block. Yes, I know that gives you even more options from which to choose. If you had studied statistics, you could tell me how many options that gives you. Suffice it to say that the number of options is in the thousands. Apologies—I just told you to limit your choices. I can't hide the truth—designing or redesigning your better business architecture is a creative and iterative process. The good news is that you don't actually need to know how many choices you have. The even better news is that understanding statistics is not required to build a better business architecture. But just in case you were feeling inadequate because you don't have a background in statistics, it's good to know that few entrepreneurs even have an MBA, so you're not alone. I certainly don't. In fact, I have a Masters of Fine Arts. That and two dollars will get me on the subway in New York City.

What is required to design your new business architecture? A firm grasp on what business you'd like to be in. If you're going to build a franchise model in a particular market, or use the train-the-trainer building block in a particular area of expertise, or create a better mousetrap for a particular industry, then commit to being in that business. You might change tactics or strategies to succeed in this marketplace, but you should be willing to commit longterm to the market you choose. That's one of the ways you send a signal to that market (your current and potential clients and customers) that you're absolutely serious about serving them for as long as they'll have you. If something is not working—a marketing strategy or a product launch—change tactics until you know how to succeed; but don't give up on the market or the building blocks you've chosen. You can't succeed at this by trying franchising for a few months and then switching over to licensing and then dabbling for a bit in network marketing. Commit to your market and the structure of building blocks through which you are going to serve that market, and stay flexible and open to opportunity until the business architecture is fully realized.

All of this is not to say that you shouldn't consider the implications of different options in the beginning. In fact, I'd like you to consider a few different scenarios for your new business architecture—what's called set-based planning (or scenario planning). This way you can compare variables of what each will probably look like as it's rolled out. What you want to avoid is making architectural decisions on the fly, as you are rolling the plan out.

It may seem like I am contradicting myself. Earlier, I suggested that too much choice can be demotivating and that you should choose quickly. Just now, I suggested that you plan in sets—that you consider different scenarios for your new business architecture. So, yes, I am saying two possibly contradictory things. I want you to plan in sets (consider multiple scenarios) *and* choose to work on the business model that you believe will be satisfactory—all the while developing the skills necessary to realize your new model.

Before you get frustrated, consider this: A June 2007 article by Roger Martin in the *Harvard Business Review* titled "How Successful Leaders Think" suggests that leaders "share a somewhat unusual trait: They have the predisposition and the capacity to hold in their heads two opposing ideas at once." I'm asking you to be such a leader. The article says that "this process of consideration and synthesis can be termed *integrative thinking*. It is this discipline—not superior strategy or faultless execution—that is a defining characteristic of most exceptional businesses and the people who run them." (The italics are my addition.) Watch for that word *integrate:* integrate business building blocks, integrate thoughts.

One more caveat—this idea may bring to mind Douglas Adams's Electric Monk from the *Dirk Gently's Holistic Detective Agency*, a time-traveling electric monk whose systems were malfunctioning from trying to hold too many conflicting ideas in his head at one time, or the Orwellian double-think concept in the book *1984.* If so, let me clarify. Integrative thinking does not mean believing in fundamentally contradictory ideas at the same time. It is not about being a hypocrite, saying one thing and doing the opposite. Rather, it means exploring the apparent contradictions between ideas and finding the ways in which many ideas, in fact, can be woven together to generate a larger idea. More than 60 years ago, F. Scott Fitzgerald suggested that the sign of an intelligent person is "the ability to hold two opposing ideas in mind at the same time and still retain the ability to function." Are you such a person?

Believe me, I know, your typical mode for business initiatives may be to roll things out as you go, to learn in action (or "figure it out on the go"). You might have heard this problem-solving method described as a Cartesian approach, after the mathematician Descartes, who said, "So long as we avoid accepting as true what is not so, and always preserve the right order of deduction of one thing from another, there can be nothing too remote to be reached in the end, or too well hidden to be discovered." In other words, step-by-step will always get us there. I respectfully (it is Descartes after all) disagree.

You can, theoretically, run your business this way. "I'll do step 1, see how it turns out, then do whatever step 2 should be, given what happened in step 1." Or you could try to go step-by-step after planning every single step in advance. In either case, this kind of planning will result in enormous waste and lost opportunities.

I subscribe to learning in action. Learning in action is an important principle for doing big things in the world, but it cannot entirely replace or be a substitute for systematic thinking and planning in sets (scenario planning), rather than in pieces (step-by-step or so-called Cartesian). Again, can you hold two contradictory thoughts in your head at the same time? For the record, I don't think Descartes thought that step-by-step was a substitute for planning ahead or scenario planning either. It's just one quote that's been used to one end.

Remember, the significant problems we have cannot be solved at the same level of thinking with which we created them. One of my primary objectives in this book is to help you steer clear of planning one piece at time. In fact, that's why I asked at the beginning of the book that you read the whole book through once, so you see the complete picture, so you can plan the whole process before starting. I want to help you understand that building your business architecture as much in advance as possible allows you to be much more focused and targeted in your approach. You can determine what you want to pursue and plan in advance how you intend to fully realize your pursuit. Advance building is also a wonderful way to mitigate your risk. More can happen than will happen, but you need to be prepared for it all. So, consider multiple options or scenarios, but stick by your choice once it's made and adjust according to market conditions. As you get bigger, planning ahead becomes ever more important; plan in sets, rather than pieces.

To that end, I'd like to help you create a set of options to consider— a set of options that will be satisfactory—rather than trying to find the one ultimate architecture for your business, which may not exist. It's more likely that there are a number of scenarios or different architectures that will allow you to go beyond booked solid, each one offering you the opportunity for satisfaction (and success).

One of the best ways to stay on track with a project is by making sure that the customers are involved in the development of the new business initiatives. Your new architecture will be all the more remarkable if you involve customers from the outset. You shouldn't create, produce, or innovate in a vacuum. For example, I developed the content for this book during a coaching program with my clients. I was able to work *in* my business while working *on* my business. And, I was able to adapt, edit, and, most importantly, improve the content for this book (and the coaching program) by creating it in real time with real paying customers. In the construction and design field, Hal calls this Target-Value Design (TVD). TVD is a way for designers to engage in the design conversation concurrently with the customers and the contractors. It is based on five premises, which I'll paraphrase (and collapse) into four premises here:

1. First, estimate before you design. In other words, don't create a detailed design and then estimate whether the resources exist to execute it. Rather, know what resources you have, and design based on estimates of what you have.
2. Second, know what's feasible before you start. As Hal puts it, "Design for what is constructible." Don't design first and then determine whether something can actually be built.
3. Third, design together, from the beginning. Instead of holing up in a room alone and designing a solution, which then gets reviewed, work together with your customers or clients (and team) to define the issues and produce decisions. Then go design.
4. Fourth, don't narrow your options too early. As you are developing different scenarios, stay flexible. This is where it counts. Don't limit your choices too early. At the same time, don't wait too long to make choices either.

Keep these TVD premises in mind as you move forward with designing your new business model. You may also consider cross-appropriation (copying or imitating the way something is done by others in a different setting or industry) as a means to developing a new business architecture for your particular industry. If you see a business model or building block in another industry or field that fits perfectly into the structure you're creating, then co-opt it and make it your own. There's nothing wrong with that. Some of the most successful businesses copy liberally from their competitors and other industries.

The Toyoda family (no, that's not a typo; their name has a "d" and the company ended up with a "t") started out with a loom production company. They were among the first to develop the automatic loom. It was the son of the founder who decided to make the switch to cars. He then made a trip to the United States, where he toured the Ford factories and saw assembly lines in action. He realized that he could not produce an inventory as large as Ford's was because he didn't have enough resources, that is, money. But he had also toured the U.S. supermarkets (something that didn't exist in Japan at the time) and the just-in-time (JIT) stocking system made just as big an impression on him as the assembly lines had. His idea, copied from Ford and the supermarkets, was to use the assembly line but to operate it using JIT principles so that cars were only made when ordered.

Toyoda cross-appropriated and improved on the things he saw in the United States to create Toyota's unique production system. Please note that I'm not talking about stealing intellectual property or patented technology. That's profoundly unethical, not to mention illegal. And, please, remember that just because I haven't mentioned a particular building block here doesn't mean that it's not a good way to do business or won't work for you or your market. Most successful entrepreneurs cross-appropriate and create new subworlds, so to speak.

You can also think of a cross-appropriating business building block as choosing from diverse practices to create a new business architecture for your industry, the way that Ray Kroc revolutionized the hamburger business by cross-appropriating assembly-line-like manufacturing processes while, at the same time, his business partner was cross-appropriating real estate development practices by turning McDonald's into a significant property-holding company, which just so happened to be the secret to McDonald's early success. I know you thought it was the Happy Meals. Me, too. Not even close. It was the cross-appropriation of real estate development strategies that was key to helping McDonald's get through the dip during the start-up period where profits from franchisees were nominal, at best. Turns out that McDonald's is in the real estate business, big time, not just the burger business.

But enough about other people's successes. Let's get to you. I certainly don't expect that you will or should complete the design of multiple new business architectures in this one chapter, or even this week or this month. Again, it's the reason I want you to read the entire book and then come back to do your planning and design. Take time to make decisions—to be truly thoughtful, reflective, and futuristic. Once you choose, implement like a pro. If you're overcritical and overwhelmed, then get over yourself and get to it—choose and learn by doing. I'd rather you do something then do nothing. Use the following tool for focusing your knowledge and implementing better decision making (after you read through the entire book). For now, you may want to give it a first pass so you understand the key factors in beginning to plan your new architecture.

Creating a Set of Options for Your Future

You need a tool for narrowing and focusing your attention because it's difficult to do more than one thing at a time—a tool that, while helping you focus your attention on what you'd like to create with your new business, will also help you create multiple scenarios for your future, a set of options. So without further ado, let me introduce you to the Beyond Booked Solid (BBS) Report. It will allow you to add and subtract various building blocks and other elements to create multiple scenarios for your future. At the same time, you'll see common elements among the scenarios, which will enable you to pick out the critical skills necessary to achieve your objectives regardless of which scenario you choose to implement. Even if you don't choose one scenario today, you'll still be able to see what skills are required to go beyond booked solid. And you can start acquiring and/or improving those skills tomorrow. The BBS Report is your planning tool.

It will help you focus your knowledge for better decision making, and it will help you develop new policies. Meaning, it will help you and your team stay focused on what you're going to do.

The BBS Report is based on the principles and practices behind Toyota's A3 Report, a tool the company uses to propose solutions to problems, to update status on ongoing projects, and to report results of information-gathering activity. I've retooled it for our purposes here. Few companies in the world excel at continuous improvement on a corporatewide basis like Toyota. The A3 Reports get their name from the international designation for the paper size used to print them; A3 paper is about 11.7 × 16.5 inches, which is roughly equivalent to twice the size of standard letterhead (8½ × 11) paper in North America.

Just like the A3 Report, the BBS Report should be printed on a single sheet of paper. Why only one sheet of paper? To keep things simple. It works well for presenting the essential elements of a single idea and still has enough information to allow you to make a decision about it. Furthermore, you can focus on one part of the report at a time, while still being able to see the whole. The guiding principle is to include whatever essential information creates a complete picture of the issue at hand, while eliminating everything else.

Elements of the Beyond Booked Solid Report

The BBS Report analyzes a problem—the fact that you are booked solid (or on the way to being booked solid)—and then presents a suggested course of action. Our goal is to make the problem and its possible solutions more visible. The BBS report includes:

- *Title of Report:* Also includes your name and any other related information.
- *Theme:* One or two sentences that describe the purpose of the report (the objective you're trying to achieve).

- *Current Situation Analysis:* A description of what you observe about your current conditions. If possible, include a visual representation (drawing, picture, graph, or chart) of the current situation.
- *Root Cause Analysis:* A diagram representing the cause(s) of the problem. These might be the constraints you identify in a later chapter.
- *Alternatives:* What are the best possibilities you are considering? If working on the new architecture for your business, include a summary of attractive building blocks, and so on, including the ones you have discarded, to enrich your discussion/thought process about the possibilities.
- *Recommendations:* What would you like to do and why? (Which alternatives do you think are the best options?)
- *Future State Picture:* What will things look like after you've made these changes? (Another great place for a picture or an image.)
- *Implementation Plan:* An outline, with action items, dates, owners, costs, issues, metrics, and other items, of how the work will actually happen (Figure 6.1).

Wondering how all of this information is going to fit on one sheet of paper, even one that is 11 $\times$ 17 inches? I too, raised my eyebrows the first time I was introduced to this concept. In the words of Walt Whitman, "The art of art, the glory of expression and the sunshine of the light of letters is simplicity." If you can't keep it simple, you probably can't implement it.

The BBS Report does not require long hours or special training. You don't even need a computer to do this. A pen and paper will do. Your job is simple—to innovate and improve. This documentation process is not an added burden to getting beyond booked solid but rather a necessary part of the process. In fact, you can use this report to solve any problem that exists in your business, assuming it's solvable.

Remember, you can download your free copy of the BBS Toolkit, which includes a blank copy of the BBS Report, at www.BeyondBookedSolid.com.

Let's have a look at a sample BBS Report that I've created (Figure 6.1). I used Brandon Hartsell and his business as my example because you've already met him along the way. You'll find his full case study in Chapter 14. However, be aware that this report is my creation. In other words, I made it up. I don't know that Brandon was ever a really stressed out yogi. I do know that I have been stressed out at times while building my business, and maybe you have, too. I wanted to make this report as relevant as possible for all of us, so I took Brandon's story and added my own flourishes for the purpose of creating the most helpful sample BBS Report. I've also included some exercises after the sample report, which may help you to focus more specifically on your objectives.

If you're someone who finds it helpful to have specific questions to provoke your thinking or if you need to work through some more of the basics, I've included the following exercises. Think of it as icing on the cake or, better yet, the cherry on top. I've also provided real-world examples based on my business. I hope they're helpful.

Exercise 1

Identify and clarify your market segment and the vertical markets that you focus on within that segment, if applicable.

Here's what I've identified as my focus: I serve professional service providers. Some of the vertical markets inside this market are financial planners; fitness, wellness, and medical professionals; real estate professionals; architects; and more.

Title of BBS Report: The Leveraged Yogi

Prepared by: Michael Port imagining that he's Brandon Hartsell

Theme:

How does a private, one-on-one yoga teacher, who used to be a professional basketball player, but also has an MBA, stop trading time for money and build a more profitable and a-historical business (without having to work a lot more)?

Current Situation Analysis:

I have a decent stable of clients. Expenses are being covered and profits are OK but not outstanding. I'm working out of my living room and sometimes go to my client's homes. I'm doing all the administrative work myself and barely have time for family and personal interests. I'm not enjoying my work like I did when I started. This is how I feel:

Root Cause Analysis:

I only have one way of making money—by trading my time for an hourly rate. This mechanism for generating revenue has no scale because it can't be run by employees or contractors. I've hit the ceiling. I can't find more hours and can only slightly increase my hourly fee. Even if I did increase my hourly fee I still have to trade my time for money and can only serve a limited number of clients. This mechanism for generating revenue has no leverage. It can't expand when I'm the only one delivering services and doing all admin, etc.

Alternatives:

Instead of offering private yoga at home and in client's homes I could:

a) Open a studio and teach classes

b) Open a studio and hire others to teach classes

c) Create a new proprietary yoga method and then offer a teacher training program

d) Open a studio and then create a franchise program

Figure 6.1   BBS Report

Recommendations:

Create a business architecture that will leverage
my strengths for organization, operations, finance, and management.
Make use of the following building blocks:

1. Intellectual Property   2. Train-the-Trainer   3. Franchise

Future State Picture:

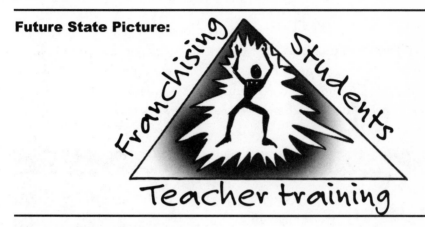

Implementation Plan:

WHAT?   **WHO?**   **WHEN?**   **WHERE?**

First: Open yoga studio and teach classes (document everything to create continuously improving system)

Second: Develop proprietary yoga method (Intellectual Property Building Block)

Third: Offer teacher training program to train teachers in the method (Train-the-Trainer Building Block)

Fourth: Have teachers teach majority of classes at studio

Fifth: Open two more studios to prove concept

Sixth: Create franchise offering and sell to most successful certified teachers already in organization

Follow up:

PLAN: **ACTUAL RESULTS:**

Figure 6.1

> **Exercise 2**
>
> Clearly articulate the value of your proposed offering to this market segment.

Here's what I've identified as my articulated value: I help people (like you) get booked solid with as many clients as they desire. Then I help them go beyond booked solid by building a better business architecture, removing constraints, and systematizing their business, which helps them make more money and work less.

> **Exercise 3**
>
> Identify the business building block, or combination of building blocks, you'll be implementing.

In my business, I use the intellectual property business model, train the trainer, and even some licensing models.

> **Exercise 4**
>
> Identify the new structure(s) for generating revenue.

My company generates the majority of its revenue through large-group coaching programs over the Internet and phone to customers all over the world. The structure allows one trainer and one administrator to serve very large groups of clients. Revenue is also derived from keynote speeches, in-person corporate trainings, private coaching with my certified coaches, and worldwide sales of books and audio products.

Exercise 5

Identify and establish the network needed to sustain (market) the business.

The network I need to sustain my business is ongoing book sales (publishing at least one new book per year), consistent speaking opportunities for me and my coaches, and an active referral base of highly satisfied customers. These are the 20-percenters. Based on the Pareto Principle, these activities amount to 20 percent of my marketing initiatives but generate 80 percent of sales.

Exercise 6

Determine what business you are currently in.

In the early days of my business, before I went beyond booked solid, I was in the consulting business doing one-on-one work with my clients.

Exercise 7

Determine what business you'll be in when you redesign the architecture of your business.

These days, I'm in two businesses:

1. The online distance-learning business.
2. The professional speaking and book-writing business.

These are the two primary mechanisms for generating revenue. The distance-learning programs are highly scalable, leveragable, and profitable. The speaking and book writing are leveragable and profitable (the speaking much more so), but neither is very scalable. Either way, I've got to be the best in the world at all three (best in the world for the people I serve).

Okay so far? That was a big chapter. Building and rebuilding the BBS Report for your business is essential. Once you've developed this roadmap for your future, you'll want to look more specifically at the resources needed to accomplish it.

7 | What Do You Need to Get There?—What You Have, What You Need

We shall never have more time. We have, and have always had, all the time there is. No object is served in waiting until next week or even until tomorrow. Keep going day in and out. Concentrate on something useful. Having decided to achieve a task, achieve it at all costs.

—Arnold Bennett

Building a bigger, better business is a matter of mastery, learning, and applying new things. Dabbling is for amateurs. Obsessing is for those who dive in head first, burn out, and then move on to something else. Also connected to this may be a shortened life span (think heart attack and other stress-related illnesses). To go the distance with your businesses, you need to become a master (not a dabbler or an obsessive) or, at the very least, pursue mastery in your chosen field. George Leonard covers the difference between mastery, dabbling, and obsessing in his book *Mastery: The Keys to Success and Long-Term Fulfillment.* Mastery is a process, not an end point. It requires continuous learning, adjustment, and adaptation to the changing world. You have already come a long way in your pursuit of mastery. Keep your energy up and keep moving ahead. You still need to build and implement your new business architecture.

Closing the Gaps

What resources do you already have that will help you reach your objectives? What resources do you need to reach your objectives? This chapter is about identifying and closing the gaps in the process, without becoming overwhelmed by the scale of the challenges you face. It's also about identifying where and when the dips may happen and preparing to get through them.

I used to be a road bike racer, strictly amateur stuff, a hobby, nothing more. As you may know from watching professionals in the Tour de France, bike racing is very often about closing the gaps. I spent a lot of time in races trying to figure out what I had and what I needed to close the gap between me and the cyclists ahead of me. I needed to assess my own energy level, the state of my equipment, and the energy level of my teammates. I needed to figure out if I was going to be the one who would pull my team and then drop back if someone else was going to pull us forward. You probably noticed that seven-time Tour de France winner Lance Armstrong spent time drafting off of his teammates (that's what it's called when a cyclist rides right behind the back wheel of the rider in front of him). Drafting off another rider takes about 30 percent less energy than being the cyclist out front. The object on bike teams is to rotate expending energy. Moreover, each racer is assigned a particular role and expends energy based on that role. It's a way of being extremely precise about the strategic distribution of resources on the bike team with the ultimate object of closing the gaps so that in the end the team leader (like Lance) is left with enough energy to surge ahead for the victory.

Building your business is the same. You can't blow all your resources at the beginning—whether they are money, people, or time. That's why you need to look ahead and assess what you have now and what you'll need to close the gaps and finish. Mastery is about closing the gaps. It doesn't happen in a day or even a week. The Tour de France is a three-week race. Only a true master can take home the victory. Even the best cyclists in the world can't finish the race. Only a rare few know how to go the distance. Closing the gaps happens over time, over the life of your business. Closing one gap may open another. But hopefully each new gap closes, bringing you to a better place. Google's engineers are constantly tweaking the search engine so it comes closer to returning exactly what a person is looking for all the time. A June 2007 article in the *New York Times* described these efforts as "the elusive quest to close the gap between often and always." Google's engineers' work will never be finished, but as they close gaps, they continue to be the masters of the search engine technology.

Knowing which gaps to close is critical. That's why choosing your new architecture and sticking with it is so important. You can't possibly close all gaps everywhere. I think of the little Dutch boy with his finger in the dam, trying to stop the leak. We only have 10 fingers. By focusing your attention on the specific new architecture you have chosen, you can master the gaps. Spread your attention too wide and you are dabbling. You will never breach the gaps. You will be overwhelmed.

Much of the work of closing the gaps is about integrating events, that is, the process by which we coordinate across projects. There needs to be someone (probably you) in charge of integrating all the pieces of the process in running the business. Integrating events can be highly complex. But if the human body can do it, then we can do it with our businesses. Think for a moment how incredible it is that we can walk and chew gum or talk and digest at the same time. Each one of those functions requires millions of different things to be happening simultaneously in our body. And yet, our body does it while we aren't even consciously thinking about it. Say thank you to your autonomic nervous system for being a master of the universe at integrating events.

We need to create the autonomic nervous system for our business—one that eventually works on its own, with your tender guidance, of course. Ultimately, you can choose to do what you wish with your time, just like I am. I'm writing this paragraph on a plane, sitting in first class, returning from a challenging and invigorating *aikido* summer camp; a car will be waiting to pick me up at the airport. I've been away from the office for almost two weeks and everything is running smoothly. Customers and clients are being well served. Money is being made. And my team is getting to do the things they love to do. All that's been required of me this week was a five-minute conversation with my operations manager. I don't mean to be cheeky. I'm just trying to point out that the pursuit of mastery in your business gives you the opportunity to pursue mastery or hobbies in other areas that you're interested in. You get to fully experience all that this life has to offer.

Your Resources

Let's make some lists, break the process down into manageable tasks. (You don't need to wait until you've read the entire book for this one. If you're ready now, go for it. If you want to wait, that's cool, too. Your choice, as always.) By the way, just like the BBS Report, you can also use these exercises any time you have an objective you want to pursue.

Exercises

Let's start with what you already know now that will help you achieve your objective (in this case, your new business architecture).

- Make a list of the information, intellectual property, or other knowledge you already have that will be useful.
- Make a list of the people you already know who can help.
- Make a list of the technology you already use or have access to that could be deployed to assist.

Now, what do you *need to know* to pursue your objective? What do you *need to learn*?

- Make a list of the information, intellectual property, or other topics you need to learn to succeed.
- Make a list of the people you need to connect with, hire, or partner with to achieve your goal.
- Make a list of the technology you need to explore to realize your vision.
- What resources do you currently *have* that will help you achieve your goal?
- Make a note of the money you can dedicate to fulfilling your objective.
- Detail the particular talents you have that will facilitate your success.
- Detail the specific skills you need to achieve your goals, and identify those skills you already have that will help you pursue your objective.
- Note the additional time you have to devote to making these changes.

(Continued)

- Record the emotional state or attitude that you have mastered or are able to sustain that is necessary to pursue your objective.

So, then, what resources do you still *need*?

- How much money, if any, do you need to create your new business architecture? Give as much detail as you can.
- Are there particular talents that you don't have that you need to fully realize this new architecture? Where might you find people with these talents to help you?
- Record the specific skills that you'll need to develop or outsource in order to be successful.
- Do you need to find time to work on creating and implementing this new architecture? If so, how much? And, don't you dare say that you can't find the time. You'll only say that if it's not important to you to succeed or if you don't believe you're capable of succeeding.
- Record any additional emotional state or disposition that you'll need to cultivate and sustain in order to create a new future.

Don't just make all these lists and throw them away. Use them to move forward. Refer back to them when you get stuck. There's a lot of work to be done. We've looked at the building blocks you'll use to design a new business architecture. We've gone through how to choose the right structure and how to keep it flexible. And now we detailed the resources we have and what we need. Designing and building your new architecture will mean undertaking a host of different projects along the way, each one with its own separate objectives. In the next chapter, we look at how you can clarify, define, and measure your objectives to better succeed at every project you take on, as you build your bigger, better business.

8

What Do You Want?—Defining and Measuring Your Objectives

Management by objectives works, if you first think through your objectives. Ninety percent of the time you haven't.

—Peter Drucker

How do you define an objective, much less measure it? What is an objective? The questions may sound trite, but the first thing you need to ask yourself as you embark on any project (like building a new or extended business architecture and going beyond booked solid) is why you are doing it. Is it because you think you ought to do the project, or is it because the project will bring you closer to your objectives? For the purposes of this book, the objective is building a bigger, better business that enables you to earn more, live more, and work less. That's the big objective, the ultimate goal. To reach that "final" objective, you will undertake dozens, maybe hundreds, of projects, each with its own objectives. Bearing in mind, of course, that even though I used that word *final,* I didn't mean it as a place you will arrive at and be done. When each project finishes, there will be another that follows. If our business architecture is our structure of fulfillment, projects are the way we undertake and fulfill individual commitments.

Countrywide Home, a mortgage lending institution, offered an investment it created from bundles of the mortgages it held, combining Class A and subprime. To make investors feel secure, Countrywide made guarantees that it would buy back some of the mortgages if the homeowners got into trouble, to protect the investors. Then a subprime mortgage crisis hit, and Countrywide couldn't (or wouldn't) make good on its promises. As of the writing of this book, I don't know how bad things will be for Countrywide. Failing to honor its commitments will at a minimum be a serious blow to the company's financial integrity and consumer credibility, not to mention the entire U.S. economy. Our businesses are sustained through making and fulfilling our commitments.

Every successful business is built on the ongoing, continuous cycle of completing one project, and then another project, and then another project. When the projects stop, the business stops. And you don't want that—unless, of course, you sell your business. Even then, the projects don't stop. They just keep going with someone else at the helm. Your objective—or at least one of your objectives—is probably to share many of the projects with others, to create a business that can nearly run itself—not without you, but without your hourly, daily, or maybe even weekly input, freeing you up for what? For more satisfying projects, of course. But don't get too drunk on the idea of not being involved in the daily activities of your business. I'm not talking about abdicating responsibility for your business. If you hate it that much, you might want to get out now. Your business is part of your life (a big part, but not all), and your life is part of your business (if you have no life, you may not be giving your business the best it deserves either). This book is to help you achieve the satisfying balance you want between those two things.

Projects and Constraints

There are two types of projects you will be doing as you work *on* your business. The first type of project is designing a new or extended business architecture that you will need to build and sustain. A new architecture might mean new offerings in your business, for example, deciding to offer seminars. How will you offer the new seminars? What will your pricing structure be? How will they be staffed and run? Will they be held at a physical venue or conducted in a virtual setting? Or maybe you've decided to franchise. How will you structure for fulfillment? You need to develop a franchise agreement that sets out the specific obligations, methods, techniques, and other things required of your franchisees.

Brandon Hartsell, cofounder of Sunstone Yoga, started out as a yoga teacher, developed his own particular teaching system and philosophy, and then designed a teacher-training program to disseminate his method. Brian Scudamore, founder and CEO of 1-800-Got-Junk?, created a franchise agreement. And Dr. Mike Berkley, director of the Berkley Center for Reproductive Wellness, enhanced his offerings by bringing in complementary fertility-related services. These were all projects that built new offerings.

> *Exercise*
>
> Make a list of the projects you need to do in your business right now. Refine the list by making a list of subprojects within each project. The lists are a good starting place. Some of the projects may end up being unnecessary. Others you haven't thought of yet will need to get done. The lists will change as you work through this book. Knowing this in advance will help you stay flexible for what the future brings. It sounds like an oxymoron, but you *can* prepare for the unexpected.

The second type of project is creating systems that remove or develop constraints. We'll look at creating systems a bit later. For the moment, what I want you to understand is that the development and/or acquisition of systems is just one more project to complete, not a whole new hurdle to overcome.

You have a list of projects. In a perfect world, we could get all the projects on our list done quickly and efficiently. Unfortunately, we don't live in that kind of world. No project comes without obstacles and constraints on our ability to just complete the project.

Let's look at constraints. A constraint instinctively sounds like something negative. Sometimes it is, sometimes it isn't. Whether a constraint is a bad thing, it is something to watch out for. You need to understand the constraints that exist to manage them effectively, and you may even want to add constraints where they will help with the completion of a project or projects. A theory of constraints was developed by Dr. Eliyahu Goldratt, in his book *The Goal*, and I learned it from Hal Macomber; so with due deference to them, I have taken their thoughts and ideas and added my own perspective. Here's my integration of all those ideas. There are generally three types of constraints:

1. *Physical Constraints:* Time and resources—there are only so many hours in the day; there is only so much money for people, space, equipment, or whatever else you might need.
2. *Policy Constraints:* A way of doing things—a typical corporate and government office policy, for example, is that everybody starts work at 9 A.M., which causes traffic jams, long lines at the muffin counter, and all sorts of other system overload reverberations. A typical family or personal policy is picking your child up from day care every Tuesday and Thursday at 2:00 P.M.
3. *Paradigm Constraints:* The way you see the world—you might believe, for example, that it takes a baker to start a bakery or that all customers complain, it's impossible to hire good people, or the first to arrive goes first.

A fourth constraint has been suggested that deals with understanding. As in, if everyone working on the project does not have a shared understanding of the objectives on the project, then that is a constraint. For simplicity, I won't go into it as fully as the other three, though I agree conceptually with the idea that alignment is critical to success and misalignment undermines your business.

Alignment, the issue of getting everyone on the same page, is part of what this whole book is about:

- Consciously choosing and understanding your business architecture is one piece.
- Choosing only projects that advance the goal of implementing the architecture is another piece.

To get there, you must ensure that the people you are working with understand the goals, that they are aligned with you and with each other. And to complete the circle, you, too, need to understand the personal goals of the people you are working with so you can identify where alignment or misalignment may exist between your separate objectives.

Let's look at our three primary constraints in a bit more detail. Believe it or not, you have control over many of these constraints.

Physical constraints may seem like the least surmountable. You can't make the day longer or print money. But if you identify exactly what the physical constraints are, you may well be able to relieve them. You don't have enough time to complete projects. Okay. Then you need to figure out how to delegate, how to unload some of the work to someone else, or how to institute systems that speed up certain tasks to make more time. Often constraints are self-imposed. Don't want to delegate to free up your time? How important is completing the project? Don't stand in the way of your own objectives. It's sad, but many people do.

Here's an example of how using a resource constraint can work to your advantage. I recently met someone who used to design Formula

One race cars (not to mention drove race cars). Of course, we talked about race car driving, which I've never done. But I do like to ride in a go-kart, and it turns out that there's quite a bit to be learned from driving underpowered toylike cars around tiny tracks. Apparently, driving a go-kart, can actually be an effective way for a race car driver to hone his skill. Why? Because it's all about skill and strategy. Unlike a real race car, where you can often rely on the power—skidding into a corner and then jamming on the gas to power out of it—in a go-kart the limited power resources mean you have to be much more skilled and strategic about how you take corners and pass people. The skills and strategies a driver acquires in the go-kart translate into superior driving skills in the powerful race cars. How can you use the limitations on your resources to your advantage, to hone your skills and strategies?

Policy constraints require a different approach. Mayor Bloomberg in New York City asked New York businesses to consider stagger-ing their work hours to relieve traffic congestion in the city. What a concept—obvious and revolutionary. Why does everyone have to be in the office at the same time for the whole eight hours of the day anyway? You aren't going to be in meetings with other people for all eight hours every day. Surely for most people, much work is done independently. Why can't 33 percent of employees arrive at 7:30 A.M., 33 percent at 8:30 A.M., and 33 percent at 9:30 A.M., or some other configuration of work hours? In fact, this kind of policy already differs substantially from city to city, country to country. A policy constraint is not necessarily negative (you may want to create policies about diver-sity or environmental impact on a project, for example), but a policy is also not carved in stone. Recognizing that policy can be changed (but only after careful consideration) is critical to understanding and relieving constraints.

Understanding policy constraints is so important that I'm going to give a few more examples. Letters used to be the norm for com-munication. Then telephones, then faxes took over. Now e-mail is ubiquitous. Some time ago, I realized that e-mail was no way for me to manage projects. All that was happening was millions of e-mails spinning around the ether in an endless loop of reply-alls that became confusing. Now I use a web-based project management tool that can be used with people inside and outside my business. The constraint to project management in my case was e-mail. I created new (positive) policy constraints using the online project management software that improved productivity and my enjoyment of working on projects.

How about the grocery checkout line? Now there's a place where policy shifts can make a big difference. How much time do we spend trying to figure out which checkout line is moving the fastest? Along came Whole Foods and turned the policy on its head. Whole Foods still has many lines, but as you reach the front of the line, you are directed to a free cashier on a rotating basis. No one slow cashier is holding up a line. Boy, do their checkout lines move fast compared to other grocery stores. Best Buy does the same thing. Of course, they are by no means the first to do this—ski resorts have been doing it with lift lines for years, they just cross-appropriated an idea from an entirely different industry and brought the concept to grocery stores.

Now let's look at paradigm constraints. Paradigm constraints are like policy constraints on steroids. A paradigm is a way we understand the world, which may be much harder to shift than a policy. A policy constraint may be a response to a paradigm constraint (for example, the paradigm is communication, the policy is to use e-mail), but a paradigm constraint runs much deeper than policy. It is the whole way we view the world. It is the first principle we start from. A paradigm can seem like a prejudice, which is broadly defined as "a preformed opinion based on insufficient information"—for example, all rich people are obnoxious, all poor people are lazy. In fact almost anytime we say "all," we're expressing something we consider to be a paradigm. And paradigms can be negative constraints. If you think all rich people are obnoxious or all poor people are lazy, you will treat people who belong to each of those groups in a certain way, without further investigation. If, for example, you set up your customer service department based on the paradigm that 99 percent of customers will complain, you will have a very specific focus in the way you structure the department, which may be counterproductive. In fact, if you are only set up to receive complaints and don't know how to deal with questions and happy customers, then you will probably end up with the complaining customers you geared up for because you'll have no mechanisms for serving the happy customers. Be careful what you wish for.

Here's another one. I'm sure you've heard the expression, "I can't find good people." It's simply not true. But if it's the way you see the world, then you have a paradigm constraint that will negatively affect your business. Why? Because you will be looking to hire the "least worst" person, instead of the best person; because you will not be thinking about how you can help people get trained and grow to be the best they can in the job. Instead you'll be thinking, "What's the compromise I'm going to have to make?" Why approach hiring like Eeyore, the naysayer in *Winnie the Pooh*?

Of course, not all paradigms are bad. It's simply that many, many paradigms are formed as prejudices, and they are based on insufficient information. Maybe the paradigm was correct at the time it was conceived, but times change and we need to constantly verify and reverify the beliefs and information underlying any paradigm to ensure that it still holds true and acts as a positive force.

Toyota is a model of how a paradigm constraint can be a positive force in a business. Toyota's first mission as a company is to serve society. Next in line are its customers, then its employees, and only then its shareholders and then itself. This is the paradigm from which everything at Toyota operates. No wonder they came out with the Prius, while other car companies lagged behind on developing hybrids. General Motors (GM) knows that Toyota is a fantastic company, so they've tried to imitate it. GM tries to use many of the same manufacturing systems that Toyota has put to such great use. But GM is simply not as successful at it. Why? Because GM doesn't operate from the same paradigm constraints. At GM, in my opinion, the first and second priorities run almost neck and neck. They are to serve its shareholders (first priority) and then itself (second priority). A distant third priority is to serve its customers, then its employees, and finally, at the bottom of the list, society. It turns out that Toyota's manufacturing systems don't work as well when they operate under different paradigm constraints.

The underlying belief system by which you operate is critical to how everything will work in your company. By the way, you'll notice that I mention Toyota a lot in the book. That's because it is a model company in many ways, which is what's made it one of the largest companies in the world and as profitable as all the other car companies combined.

Here's a nice example of working around a paradigm constraint. Lori Kliman and Heather White started Cupcakes by Heather and Lori, a successful Vancouver bakery with two locations (as of this printing), and more in the works—and they didn't know how to bake (still don't). Everyone told them they couldn't do it. They disagreed. They knew about marketing and publicity. Good bakers could be hired. In fact, they turned their backs on another paradigm, too. Pastry people are normally subject to a superior who controls the design of the pastries. Heather and Lori gave their pastry chefs design freedom. As you can imagine, what they got was a creative and happy kitchen. Two paradigms turned on their heads for the price of one. The result? Success.

Changing the way we view things, changing what we believe, is unusual and takes conscious effort (remember conscious discloser?). That's what innovation is about. You can do it. Just knowing you can do it is often enough to get you thinking. In fact, paradigm constraints are essentially just another dimension of your all-important attitude (you didn't forget about your attitude, did you?). Our belief systems (the things that we believe are paradigms) shape our attitude, and vice versa. Changing one changes the other, and the shifts in perspective will have reverberations in all aspects of our lives.

Relieving and Applying Constraints

The first constraint you have to relieve to go beyond booked solid is *you*. If you are booked solid, then you are the constraint. You have no time to do the work necessary to continue building your business. Your lack of availability is a brake on growth. I know. I've been there, thinking, *I don't have time to think about the future of my business.* Know this—if you aren't thinking about the future of your business, no one else will be and there won't be anything different in the future to look forward to.

Change, contrary to what your 13-year-old has learned from Harry Potter, doesn't happen by magic. If you treat yourself as a constraint, then you can begin to move beyond it. Then you can look at what other constraints there are to growth in your company. What are the physical, the policy, and the paradigm constraints holding you back? Identify them. Relieve them where you can. Never say, "It can't be done." Maybe in the end a constraint can't be relieved. But chances are good that once it's identified, it will be more manageable. Again, it's sad to think that many people don't believe their constraints can be removed. Entrepreneurs are different. The entrepreneurial spirit is all about finding new ways of doing things: creating a new product, offering a new service. By nature, an entrepreneur is someone who thinks, "This *can* be done." Are you an entrepreneur?

Another word about constraints—they are, as I said, not all negative. Some constraints are necessary to keep a project moving forward. Deadlines are positive constraints; without deadlines most projects would never get done. This book, for example, got done a lot faster because I knew I'd signed a contract with a fixed delivery date for the manuscript. Without the specter of my editor looking over my shoulder, this project could have easily been pushed to the back burner. A deadline is an important constraint to ensure project completion. An unreasonable deadline, or one you know you can't meet, should be an indication that you should not take on a particular project.

Customers and clients can be positive constraints. As Hal says, "The client's conditions for satisfactory completion positively constrain by giving priority or focus to project work." All business projects are done for clients, in one sense or another. They might be external clients or internal clients. You might be the client. For example, if you have your assistant implement a new project management system (the way I implemented one for my team), you are the client. If you are building a new or extended business architecture, you are the client.

This is all another way of saying—what's your objective? What projects bring you closer to it? A project should not exist without the constraint of customer necessity. Back to e-mail again for another example. I don't respond to it instantly or even within the hour, as many people do. That's because I have a policy—I respond to e-mail once a day, if that often. (Tim Ferriss, author of *The 4-Hour Workweek*, taught me that trick.) What a Luddite you might be thinking. (Luddites were members of a social movement in the English textile industry who opposed the changes of the Industrial Revolution, specifically mechanized looms. Now Luddite refers to anyone opposed to technological advances. With the pace of technology change today, it's a fun word to know because there are lots of modern Luddites.) My opposition to e-mail is the reverse of Luddism, though. I could never complete the number of projects I do if I was a slave to my e-mail, checking it every five minutes. You know what I'm talking about, don't you? Yes, I glance at what's come in during the day and if there's something important, I respond right away. But for the most part, the e-mails I receive (and likely you, too) can wait 24 hours for a response. Of course, I have a different policy for my customer help desk e-mail. That's checked every hour. E-mail is a tool, not an obligation. Use it to your advantage. Apply constraints where it is getting in the way of your productivity. Apply constraints to improve performance.

These kind of positive or helpful constraints are essential to prevent what's known as "project creep." You're starting an addition to your house. Midway through the project, you decide you just want to add a little spiral staircase here. Then you're asking the contractor, "Could we just add . . . ?" It happens. Deadlines, keeping your eye on the end customer of a project (who may be you), and rules of engagement (like e-mail habits) are all positive constraints. Think about constraints you might impose on yourself or your team to be more efficient. Again, when we talk about systems later, we'll think about how systems can be put in place both to relieve and impose constraints.

Start by thinking about what ideas you have that are inhibiting you from achieving what you want. For example, many people say, "It's impossible to get a book published." If I thought that, which I don't, that would be a constraint that was inhibiting me from achieving my objective—to write and then sell lots of copies of my books. Here's another way of thinking about it. What do you think is "normal" in your business? Maybe that's a constraint. I used to be in the acting business. In that business, it was normal to think that if you took time off you would never be able to get back in. Well, I have a friend who took several years off acting to work in business; when he went back to acting, he landed a job as one of the leads on the popular television show *Lost*. He certainly didn't let what was "normal" stand in the way of what he wanted.

Exercise

Make a list of all the things that you think are constraining you in your business. List the positive and the negative constraints in separate columns. If you are having trouble identifying the constraints, start with your objectives. What do you want? Periodically review your list of constraints, add new ones, and remove those that no longer apply.

Constraints help you stay on track with projects. I mentioned customers as a sort of constraint. Let's think more about customers, or clients, or whatever you call the end users of your services. This book is about extending/building and implementing a new business architecture that will result in a bigger, better business. The projects you engage in to reach that end goal are projects that work *on* your business. In other words, you are the customer for some of these projects. Of course, your customers will also benefit from the new architecture you put in place—if you are able to deliver better, more remarkable services.

Measuring Project Success

You need to be able to determine exactly what you are pursuing (i.e., what your objectives are) in some kind of measurable form. That way you can see immediately if you have strayed from the path. Measuring is essential to staying on track. It creates discipline and a mechanism for identifying where things are going astray. Lots of people talk about how important measurement is. The key to innovation is measuring the right things. Not all innovation is successful, is it? And measuring the right things may spell the difference. You may think, "I made 100 calls today." But is that the right measurement? Was it efficient or effective? Measuring the things that are relevant to what you are pursuing both professionally and personally is critical. Here's a sample list of the types of individual project successes you might measure in general, as you work *on* your business (your job is to be specific regarding what you're measuring):

- Specific milestones that represent the different stages of successful implementation of your new architecture—drafting a franchise agreement, identifying franchise locations, joining a social network, developing a brand logo or slogan, and so on.

- Personal fulfillment in your business—are you spending the majority of your time working in areas of your strengths? What percentage of your time is occupied by busywork or work that others could easily do?
- The success of the people with whom you work—are they meeting the performance benchmarks you set together? Are they treated the way they want to be treated?
- Marketing results—what conversion rates are you getting to your opt-in e-newsletter? What percentage of customers/clients are repeat buyers?

These are broad renderings of the kinds of objectives you will set for yourself as you go beyond booked solid. Of course, yours will be much more specific.

Exercise

Make a preliminary list of the kinds of objectives you have right now. How can you measure the success of each one?

Measuring the success of your objectives is only part of the challenge. How you measure the success of people with whom you work is essential and can be tricky. When you are measuring, you need to find the right standard. Remember the Platinum Rule? You need to know why people are working for you. What drives them? Is it for the money, or is it for another reason? Dr. Mike Berkley learned that most of the people who work in his wellness clinics are not motivated by money but rather, they want to have a purpose and want to contribute to society. What is it that the people working with you need for their own personal fulfillment in business? The people with whom you work will only be successful if they are fulfilled—just like you. In fact, according to the Gallup organization, the number-one reason that people quit jobs is because they feel like they are not making a difference in their work. Wanting to make a difference—being fulfilled—trumps money as the most decisive factor in job satisfaction. Of course, you also need to measure their success in making and meeting deadlines, designing and completing projects, and more.

Great business builders are also paying attention to what the people around them want. So, in a sense, employees are the customers of your management style. You want to meet their needs, too. You can't ensure the personal fulfillment of every person you ever work with. People are different. You need to identify the types of people who fit your organization and your philosophy, people who are predisposed to succeed in your particular environment. You can't and won't please all of the people all of the time, but you will have much more success if the people around you are succeeding, too.

One last word about measuring—beware of the paradox. I've stressed that you have to know what you want before you can get it and that you must measure the success of projects. I still hold to that. But you can't be so specific about your goals that you preclude getting something better, a paradox indeed. In the midst of all this "knowing what you want" and "measuring the success," you need to stay flexible, stay open to other, better opportunities that may present themselves along the way. Lori Kliman and Heather White wanted to open a cupcake bakery. And they did. Their goal was to make great cupcakes and supply wholesale and retail. Along the way, they got an opportunity to make a wedding cake. It wasn't what they'd planned. They hadn't known in advance they wanted to make wedding cakes. But it was a golden opportunity and they seized it. They incorporated wedding cakes into their objectives and, just like every other objective they'd set for themselves, they measured its success. Now wedding cakes are part of their standard offerings. So the paradox is defining what we want in the face of an uncertain, and unknowable, future. You can do it.

Pitfalls

I want to close this chapter by pointing out two potential pitfalls along the road to project completion. They are what Hal calls the "Two Great Wastes"™.

- Not speaking
- Not listening

They sound obvious; but, in fact, they are the two biggest dangers you face, the two things that stand most in the way of you getting what you want. What do they really mean?

Not speaking is not communicating what you need and want. We are often afraid to say what we want—out of fear of ridicule or rejection, superstition, or the simple inability to articulate what we want. If you can't articulate what you want, you will never get it. Similarly, if you are afraid to speak it aloud, you will never get it.

Not listening is giving your attention to something else and not to the project that will further your goals. Back to my e-mail again. Do I really need to check it every five minutes? How can I pay attention, that is, *listen*, to what's needed on my projects if I'm constantly distracted? Not listening sometimes masquerades as multitasking.

So, when are you multitasking, and when are you simply not paying enough attention to something? Be clear what you mean by multitasking. Is it doing e-mail while you're on the phone? That's something that might seem efficient, but likely what it really means is that you're not paying attention to the person you're on the phone with. Are you sending an e-mail related to the content of the phone call, or are you engaged in unrelated correspondence? If it's the latter, you're not listening. However, you will always have more than one thing to do. You will need to work through things on your to-do list somewhat simultaneously, which is not to say that you will be doing two things at the same exact moment. Rather, your aim is to "batch" everything you do (thank you to David Allen, author of *Getting Things Done: The Art of Stress-Free Productivity*, for this great idea). Slice tasks up into small pieces of action. For example, check e-mail once or twice a day for half an hour, instead of checking it all day long at frequent intervals. Divide your to-do list into different categories. Everything that can be done in less than two minutes, do right away. Another category might be "everything that is actionable, but waiting for someone else or something else." There should be a category for "actionable, but takes longer than two minutes" and probably a "read and review" category. Throughout the day, you may be working in batches on items in each of these categories—that's multitasking. Be sure it doesn't lead you into not speaking or not listening.

If we don't speak and/or we don't listen, it leads to waste and unfinished projects. Why? Because integrating events, the process by which we coordinate across projects, becomes difficult, if not impossible. Projects are both independent and dependent. A small business owner will face major business breakdowns if coordination falls apart between the various independent contractors and vendors who are essential to the business. And if you haven't defined your objectives and you aren't measuring the outcomes, then you might not notice fast enough that things are falling apart or how badly.

Bear in mind from the outset what you want, why you want it, what the constraints are (positive and negative), and how you will measure whether you got what you wanted. Awareness is half the battle. Once you begin to define your objectives, identify constraints, and measure outcomes more intentionally, you will be surprised by how much more smoothly things will flow.

9 | Projects—How to Get Things Done

The work of organizations is making and keeping commitments.
—*Fernando Flores*

Just as a business is emergent, so are projects. After all, what is a business but a series of successfully completed projects? So it follows that as with your business, the future course of a project is uncertain. Even if you create a very clear outcome for a project, you can't know for sure that you'll achieve the particular outcome until the project is complete. Don't give up or throw up your hands in despair at the uncertainty. It's the reason that many people don't attempt to do big things. They're too afraid to take on something big when they can't determine an exact outcome. It's a classic catch-22. Often the very people who are perfectionists, control freaks we might also call them, and who therefore think that the projects they complete will be the best can't actually complete projects, much less get started, in many cases. However, you *can* create circumstances that will help you navigate a project to its intended result. You might not end up exactly where you intended, but if you follow a few simple rules (thank you to Hal Macomber for the original versions of these rules, which I've

93

made liberal use of), then you may end up with a far better result than you originally envisioned. I'll give you the list of rules, and then we'll look more closely at each one:

Simple Rules for Getting Things Done

- Collaborate.
- Adopt practices for exploring a variety of perspectives.
- Coordinate meticulously.
- Listen generously.
- Build relationships intentionally.
- Have clear intentions.
- Develop habits of commitment making and fulfilling.
- Tightly couple learning with action.
- Call on your talents.
- Bring your passion to the project.
- Embrace uncertainty.
- Have a compelling story for your project.

Collaborate

I mean it. Really collaborate. Work with others. At the earliest possible moment, bring people into a project, even as it is just developing. If you work with others, you should accomplish greater things than you could alone. If this is a tough rule to follow or if you are hesitant to involve other people, ask yourself whether you are committed to having something truly great or just to getting it done your way—it's not the same thing. Make it your rule to plan with those people who will be part of the project team. Don't wait until the project has gone south to get their help. Start out with everyone on board. Continue collaborating as you work through the project. Bring others in at the earliest possible moment to help shape the outcome of the project. Remember, it's difficult to determine a result, and often the harder you try to force an outcome, the more likely you are to quash creativity. However, if you really collaborate, using these rules for producing remarkable projects, your project partners will help you create something far better than you could alone.

Adopt Practices for Exploring a Variety of Perspectives

We think we see what's there, but we don't. We see what we expect to see. We see what we already think or believe exists. Instead, make it your habit to inquire as to what others see, how other people view a situation. Your single perspective locks your disclosive space (sounding familiar?); it is not the ultimate or only truth. It's your job (particularly as a manager) to see from others' perspectives. Whoever said that we needed to walk a mile in another person's shoes to fully understand them was onto something. You will see more together, and together, you can see new things, new ways of acting and being. If I wanted to say this in a fancy way, then I'd say: *Together you can disclose new subworlds.*

Coordinate Meticulously

A project is an ever-evolving network of commitments. Keep that network activated by tending to the critical conversations. Be sure to integrate events. See that people make clear requests, undertake commitments that have completion dates, and share opinions that advance the purpose of the project. Without attention to those critical conversations, the project will drift. When you're doing a project with one person, maybe you can coordinate effectively via e-mail. Find what works for you. As I mentioned, I've found that trying to manage a project via e-mail results in hours of time and energy wasted. As your projects grow in scope and size, you will need a better way to coordinate and manage all of the project activities.

Listen Generously

It's not often that people feel like they're able to say what they want in the moment, either because they don't feel like they're invited to speak or because, even if they may speak, sometimes it's hard to articulate, in the moment, just what they think or want. For the most part, people are well-intended. Give them the benefit of the doubt. Take the time to listen. Ask questions. Seek others' opinions. And while you're at it, don't be so harsh on yourself.

Build Relationships Intentionally

Often project teams come together as relative strangers or at least strangers to working closely together. Some might even say that projects work better this way because there is more opportunity to learn from one another. However, to do great work—innovating, learning, collaborating—it takes a group of people who like and care for each other. Don't leave that to chance. Start your projects by building relationships among team members. A shared understanding is key. Make sure everyone understands the goal of the project and is invested in its success. Quickly remove performers who do not or cannot care for others on a project. Quickly remove performers who are not and will not invest in the success of the project. There are too many people who would love to do something special with you for you to waste time with those who won't.

Have Clear Intentions

As the saying goes, "If you don't know where you're going, any road will take you there." The same thing applies to doing projects. In order to have clear outcomes, you need to have clear intentions about what you want to accomplish. Your intention is made up of your passions, your talents, your contributions, the commitments you undertake, and the promises you fulfill. Define your project in as much detail as possible. But, as with all creative pursuits, flexibility is essential. Leave room for change, expansion, and possibly a new direction. This will create the most collaborative and exciting environment within which you can create.

Develop Habits of Commitment Making and Fulfilling

This is my favorite rule and I implore you . . . plead with you . . . beg you to take it to heart. Progress depends on the successful fulfillment of promises. Create a routine that is appropriate for the project, which requires the team to come together and to undertake promises to one another. The work that I promise to complete today allows you to start your task tomorrow. The downfall of not fulfilling my obligation is one breakdown after another. In fact, our reputations are built on our ability, or lack thereof, to make commitments and fulfill them, as is the future success of our businesses. There are people who are great at making commitments but not great at fulfilling them. When that happens, not much gets done, and they don't get picked to participate on a project team again. Others don't make commitments. Yet, without commitments in the first place, not much gets done, and they don't get asked to participate again either. The good news is that projects are a perfect venue to develop and improve habits of commitment making and fulfilling. I should note that commitments can, and sometimes should, be renegotiated. That's perfectly natural. Things change. But if renegotiating promises becomes the norm, then not much gets done, at least not in a timely fashion. And, you guessed it, you don't get asked to participate again.

Hal suggests that "Nothing works better than a 10- to 15-minute daily coordination and commitment management conversation. Each team member assesses how they are doing fulfilling promises. They report complete when done or make revised promises when needed.

They also make new promises at the appropriate time on a project. They finish by asking for help or offering help to others. A four- to seven-person team can have this conversation in less than 15 minutes."

Tightly Couple Learning with Action

One of the things that keep people from getting on with their projects is that they think they need to know everything before they start, instead of learning in action. As Eric Hoffer, an American philosopher, says, "In a time of drastic change it is the learners who inherit the future. The learned usually find themselves equipped to live in a world that no longer exists."

The future belongs to the learner, not the learned. Projects are wonderful opportunities to learn. Most teams look for lessons learned after a project is completed, often called a postmortem. But at that point the project is dead, just as the term *postmortem* implies. Sure, learning from the project might help avoid mistakes on the next one, but if you learn while doing, you can do things you've never done before. Remember TWI, the Training Within Industry instruction method we talked about earlier? TWI is all about learning in action. It creates a continuous learning loop and, organizations that use TWI tend to be learning organizations, companies that are constantly looking for ways to improve.

Toyota is the classic example of a company successfully using TWI. In fact, Japanese companies in general use TWI more than U.S. companies. Why is that? After all, it was the American TWI staff who taught the Japanese TWI after World War II. But then it seems that U.S. companies got a bit too arrogant and stopped thinking they needed to learn something, or maybe prosperity set in, whereas continuous learning is much more in the Japanese business nature. They even have a word for it—it's called *kaizen* (I used that expression earlier in the book). TWI largely survived as a Japanese corporate practice, not an American one, although it may be making a comeback in the United States.

When business ideas are generated in a more communitarian fashion, an environment is created in which ideas and mistakes are analyzed without laying blame on any one individual. By contrast, if ideas tend to belong to an individual, then mistakes are generally laid at one person's doorstep. People are loath to point out something that's going wrong for fear of taking the blame. But if you play the blame game, then problems aren't fixed midstream. Instead, they are identified only in postmortems as something to watch for "next time." Next time is too late.

At Boeing, a "plus delta" review of the status of projects is undertaken at the end of every meeting. Delta is the symbol used in math and science to indicate change, positive or negative. So a "plus delta" review looks at the things that have happened or changed on a project to move it closer to completion (the positive, or plus, things). It's not a process of self-criticism. It's a process of reviewing what is producing value on a project and what is reducing value. It maximizes the former, while eliminating the latter. It's about fixing the problems on the go, not about finding the fall guy. In agile software development, this is called a retrospective. Toyota, of course, does it too, probably better than anyone.

Learning while doing is not just for big companies; every business, no matter the size, will benefit from the continuous examination of the status of its projects and every other aspect of the business. Not only will this ensure that a project goes more smoothly, but it will also ensure that a project gets started. Most people get held up because they think they have to know something before they start something. Or they wait for perfection—they keep sharpening the saw but never actually cut anything.

As Ron Quintero, founder of My Resource Center, Mortgage Leaders Edge, Debt Advisory Alliance, and Finance This Home, says, he didn't have all the answers when he started, nor for that matter does he now. He let the people he worked with know that he didn't have all the solutions before starting a project. He told them, "We're going to learn this together," and they did.

Make it a habit to incorporate learning loops in all your project activities. That may mean starting before you feel quite ready, being willing to risk that the next steps will become clearer as you go along. Learn by doing. Learn in action. But keep looking at what you've learned as you go. Don't wait until the end to see if it all added up to enough new learning. I can't tell you how often to look at what you're doing. It might be daily, or weekly, or even monthly, depending on the size of the project and the intensity of the demands. It just needs to be often enough that you can correct mistakes as you are going along, but not so often that you stop the actual flow of the project because you are spending so much time looking at it instead of doing it. Your team will appreciate learning in action. Your customers will benefit from it. And best of all, it will make your job easier and more fun.

Call on Your Talents

Working on a project of any sort is the perfect venue for showcasing your talents. *Talents* are those gifts that are innate to the person you are, whereas skills are things that are learned. When you use your talent, you do better work. Avoid taking on responsibilities and tasks that fall outside the scope of your natural talents. And don't let your project team do it either. As the project manager, it's your responsibility to make sure that no one on the project takes on responsibilities in areas outside their talents. It's okay to learn a new skill while working on a project—in fact, it's how you learn new skills—but you'll learn much faster if you are hardwired with the talent to excel at that skill.

Devour Marcus Buckingham's book on the subject of exploiting your strengths—*Now, Discover Your Strengths* and *Go Put Your Strengths to Work*. And, as a leader, bear in mind what Jim Collins, author of *Good to Great: Why Some Companies Make the Leap . . . and Others Don't*, said about seats on the bus. It's not enough to hire the best and the brightest to get them on the bus. You need to be sure that you have each person in the right seat on the bus, that is, good people still need to be in the right positions, doing the work that exploits their strengths.

Bring Your Passion to the Project

Passion is a requisite for producing remarkable projects. You are not likely to do a project that others are going to remark on if you don't engage your passion. As with anything, when we're creating something new, we're faced with problems, seemingly insurmountable barriers, and circumstances that are out of our control. During these times, it is our passion and personal investment in the project that carries us through to completion. Passion goes beyond attitude or disposition. It is that extra zeal that all truly successful people have. If you're not passionate about a project you're working on, ask why. If you can't get passionate about it, you might want to reconsider doing it or find someone else who is passionate about it to do it. If you don't believe in something but you continue working on it, I can almost guarantee you that it will not go well. At a minimum, you will expend two to three times as much energy and effort as you should to complete the project. In worst-case scenarios, you will botch it before finishing.

Embrace Uncertainty

Expect the unexpected. There is far more that we don't know and can't know than what we can anticipate. Be resilient to what your project throws at you. Anticipate that your team will learn something along the way that can and should change what you have promised and how you can deliver on your promises. And when you face a setback—we all do sometime or another—review the other rules for how you can work your way out of it.

Have a Compelling Story for Your Project

Projects never go the way you expect they are going to go! (See the previous section—Embrace Uncertainty.) Keeping your passion and your focus depends on telling and retelling the story of your project. Your story is about why this project matters to you and why it is important for others. On a grander scale, it is your vision and purpose rolled into one. It will become increasingly important as you face problems, setbacks, or any type of project breakdown. You can always go back to your story—the underlying reason why you undertook the project in the first place. Storytelling is a tool of leadership and the way you engage others in your project. It's the way you maintain your mood when things go wrong. Being able to articulate and rearticulate the story of the project is essential.

Psychology professor Dan McAdams' book *The Redemptive Self: Stories Americans Live By* talks about the way we tell stories about ourselves, in particular our life story. Research like McAdams' and a 2005 study done by psychologists at Columbia and the University of California, Berkeley, and published in the journal *Psychological Science*, have shown that when we tell our life stories, we are really just telling ourselves who we are and why. McAdams found, for example, that successful people often tell a life story characterized by overcoming adversity, connections with others, and a belief in the future. In fact, the narrative themes we choose when we tell our life story may well be driving factors in our behavior. After all, our life story is just one interpretation or retrospective reconstruction. And it's been shown that people's life stories may and can change radically over time, even descriptions of the same events. We have the ability to change these stories, which are fundamental to who we are and what we become. Never discount the power of the stories you tell about your projects. Stories articulate why a project is important to everyone involved, and they keep the project on track. You are the storyteller of your business innovation. You write the story. What's your story?

Exercise

List five projects you are working on right now. Why are you doing them? Why does each project matter to you? Why should it matter to others working with you or in your life? Who else cares about the outcome of the project?

Playing Catch with Hal

We're going to go back for a moment to the first rule I mentioned in the list—collaborate. Accumulating another debt to Hal's thinking, let's look at what he calls "Let's Play Catch," which I'll just call collaborating or working with other people. Success in a project depends on the success of the team. So we need to focus on how well people are working together, which means focusing on others' success, not just our own (that Platinum Rule has many forms).

Working together is nothing more than a continuous conversation. Conversations are like playing catch. You can play catch (or have conversations) with people of varying skill levels. The method of the game is continued play. Never stop the conversation. Keep talking to each other. The primary strategy is to throw so the other person can catch. Speak so the other person can listen. Listen so the other person can speak. The tactics are to adjust behavior based on recent success or failure. The conversation guides action. The game has rules. I know, now I'm giving you rules within rules, but bear with me. The rules integrate so well together that you won't even notice. I promise. In fact, you may feel like it repeats some of what I've said earlier, and that's good. These are key things to understand as you build your business, and they bear repeating in different contexts so you can see them from all angles.

Here goes: the rules for playing catch, or the rules for collaborating— the rules within the rules. And remember, sometimes you are the project manager, the leader. Sometimes you are part of the project team. Sometimes you are the client. Teach everyone with whom you do projects how to play Hal's game of catch:

Be Clear about What You Want

- Specify the conditions of satisfaction. What has to happen for the project to be a success?
- Include all the ingredients of the completed work product. Don't gloss over any aspect of the project. Be clear up front about each element necessary for completion.
- Use nouns and adjectives, not verbs and adverbs. People working on projects often speak about what they're doing without talking about what they will accomplish. The doing is not as important as the completion. Start all planning sessions with a conversation around outcomes (using nouns and adjectives). Check that those outcomes meet your client's conditions of satisfaction. Remember, you may be the client.
- Describe what you will be completing so it can be witnessed. A task is not complete until its completion is witnessed by the client.
- Be sure that what you want to complete is relevant to the client. This seems even more relevant when you see yourself as the client, doesn't it? Establishing a context for the project team helps provide a basis for taking better care of you. Why something is being done can shape how a person goes about the task. Reasons inform actions. Context is essential to ensuring everyone gets what they want.

Ask for What You Want

- We rarely get what we don't ask for.
- Ask for all of what you want, not just what you think you can get, or what you think will be acceptable to others, or what you think you can live with if you can't have everything.

- Be open to other conditions of satisfaction after you've been clear about what will satisfy you. Negotiating the conditions of satisfaction is a normal part of getting things done. Decide if getting something done your way is more important than creating something better with others.

Ask People to Ask Questions

- The principle source of not getting what you want (other than not asking for it) is assuming people understand what we ask them to do. Never assume. You know how the rest of the saying goes. Clarity is essential. If you have trouble being clear, ask others to help you clarify your requests by asking clarifying questions.
- Encourage everyone, particularly new people on your team, to explore your conditions of satisfaction so they know exactly what you expect. As mentioned before, be open to adjusting your expectations.
- If you don't get questions, then ask your own questions. Incite conversation. It's rare that a lack of questions is a good sign. Usually it's a sign of confusion, lack of engagement, or, worse yet, that the team doesn't care about the outcome.

Invite People to Offer Alternatives

- Say what you want, and then ask if there is something else that could be better. This can't be a fake question. Be open to alternatives. (Remember our discussion of being a conscious discloser).
- Adopt a mood of inquiry with the project team to explore alternatives. Remember how important it is to determine what disposition (mood) is required to reach your objectives. Dr. Daniel Goleman, author of *Primal Leadership: Learning to Lead with Emotional Intelligence*, links the mood state of a team to future earnings. He concludes that companies that enjoy a

positive mood state are more likely to succeed due to performer engagement and resulting customer satisfaction. (The same holds true for internal business projects—projects that work *on* your business.)

- Make team building an opportunity to tap into the expertise, talents, and interests of performers. It can't be all about you.

Be Clear When You Want It

- Don't leave people guessing when you want the task completed. Again and again, clarity, clarity. If you don't set dates for task, milestone, and project completion, you don't have a project. You just have some ideas and a lot of work, which rarely gets done.
- To gain a wholehearted commitment to the deadline, be open to suggestions of different schedules.
- When you have a lot of flexibility, ask others to set the due date. In that way they will feel even more bound by the deadline.
- Document everything. It is important to have an observer in your life—someone or something that can notice change. The same is true for your project work. In order to observe the progress of a project, document everything. If a tree falls in the forest but no one hears it, did it make a sound? Sure, but no one knows to get the wood chipper fired up and ready to go. Use a tool (software, hardcopy, whatever) for managing projects. Which tool you use is not as important as how well you use it.

Dealing with the Inevitable

Even following these simple rules, project breakdown will occur. It will come in many different forms: People will disappoint, promises will be broken, and real-world circumstances will change. Project breakdown is normal. In fact, it's virtually guaranteed when you are working toward producing remarkable results. In offering you my version of Hal's Simple Rules for Getting Things Done, my intention is to encourage you to think about the work in your business as a series of projects—where sometimes you are a project manager, sometimes a team member, sometimes a client—with specific milestones and tasks and people who will achieve the milestones and fulfill the tasks.

One of the most difficult aspects of building a bigger, better business is taking yourself out of the equation as the primary project person. The situation is only compounded when you try to complete a whole slate of projects through e-mail, phone conversations, and your already overloaded short-term memory. The more you try to track your projects with your mind, the less mindful you are and the more mindless your work becomes. How could you possibly manage commitments made, find opportunities for learning, and measure performance without help from somewhere? Systems. Systems. Systems. We're coming to that.

Observe the Change You've Wrought

Building a business that can and will go beyond booked solid is not an overnight process. It will never be, "What I did over the weekend." Not just your business but you and probably the people around you will undergo enormous change. Without an outsider observing the changes, you may not even realize how far you've come. I mentioned earlier that I'm a student of *aikido*, martial art founded in Japan by Morihei Ueshiba, 1883–1969. My teacher (*sensei*) observes how I change in my practice. He asks new things of me when he sees sufficient improvement. When he sees breakthroughs, he asks more of me. When he sees breakdown, he responds accordingly. Frequently, I have been as surprised by a promotion as by a scolding. I have not been as aware of changes, both positive and negative, as my teacher because I'm so focused on my day-to-day practice of *aikido* and, of course, all the distractions of life.

My teacher has much more perspective and experience than I do. He can see changes I haven't yet fully assimilated. He can see things I need to improve. He can also point out and reward improvements.

An outside observer of the changes is best, a business coach, for example. But you are your own observer, too. Through time, we change as observers/disclosers. Writing in a journal provides the opportunity to notice how you have changed. You will never truly see or understand changes you've made unless there is an observer of the change to record it (you or a third person).

Change is coming. Once you've read this book and started to internalize the content, you'll likely start making changes (big and small) to the way you do things. Start the record now. Begin a journal. Earlier I said that you ought to read this book through once to get an overview of where we were going and to see the road map in full. And I stand by that strong recommendation. This is not a step-by-step process. But keeping a journal is one thing I'd like you to start now. Write a little every day. But first . . .

Exercise

Write your autobiography—the autobiography of your business, that is, not of your high school prom or all the pets you've had over the years. Make it about 15 pages long. If it is too short, there won't be enough for you to observe changes; too long and you'll be mired in writing instead of getting on with building a bigger, better business. Go ahead. Pick up your pen, or fire up your keyboard. When it's done, set it aside. This is not the same thing as your journal. This is your story today, before you start building the bigger, better business. When you have achieved your objective or at least a major interim objective (since ideally there will always be more objectives to reach) for example, your new architecture is in place, write your autobiography again. Then compare the two. Observe the change. Repeat at intervals.

Phew. We've covered an enormous amount of ground in the chapters so far. I've asked you to adopt a specific attitude and to open yourself up to a host of new ideas and new ways of being. I have shown you a range of business building blocks you might use to design a new or extended business architecture. I have taken you on a whirlwind tour of how to do projects and the obstacles and constraints you may face. I've given you rules for getting things done and rules within those rules for how to collaborate with others.

Chances are that you can already feel the winds of change blowing you forward. Hoist the sails. Fire your engines. Think in terms of whatever metaphor gets you going. It's time to do some systems thinking. Huh? That sounds so . . . so . . . uninspiring. Not so at all. Systems are what are going to make it all possible. Without systems in place, you will never find the time to work *on* your business, while working *in* your business, while, of course, *working on yourself.* Systems are the *how* that gives you time for the *why* (and lots of other stuff, too).

10

Systems—
A Business That
Runs Itself

It must be remembered that there is nothing more difficult to plan, more doubtful of success, nor more dangerous to manage, than the creation of a new system. For the initiator has the enmity of all who would profit by the preservation of the old institutions and merely lukewarm defenders in those who would gain by the new ones.

—Niccolú Machiavelli

Did you read the title of this chapter and think, *Finally, this is the part I've been waiting for, the part where I learn how my business can run itself.* I hate to disappoint you, but that's simply not possible. You can leverage more and work less, but there is no such thing as a business that runs itself. Sure, it's an expression people use; and yes, it is possible to have highly automated systems taking care of many aspects of your business. But you will always need people. People need to be involved in creating the systems. *That's just work up front,* you might be thinking.

111

True, once a system is created, people (i.e., you) may need to be less involved, but I only said *less*. People will always be needed to execute and maintain the systems, to tweak them for new functionality, and, most importantly, to innovate and to figure out what new things the system needs to do to stay current and competitive. You aren't abdicating your business to a machine or a system. You are creating a support structure that frees you to spend more time (all your time) on the things you love doing. Systems are what enable you to work *on* your business while you're working *in* your business and *on yourself*. Systems are *how* we reduce waste in our businesses so they can grow.

How much time do you waste? How do you even know? Maybe you are the most efficient person on the planet and never waste one minute. In that case, you can skip this chapter. For all the rest of us, let's start with a simple calculation. How much time do you spend looking for a phone number you put somewhere . . . but where is it when you need it? It hasn't quite made it into your address book yet. The business card is just here, or there, underneath this paperweight, or that one. And how about passwords that are so secret even you don't know what they are, except that it's your password and you need it to get into a web site and you can't remember the clever spot where you hid it. Then there's the I-just-know-it's-here-somewhere moments when you are looking for that old proposal, because it's so juicily similar to the one you have to write today and it would save you so much time if you could just put your hands on it. If only . . . but you can't.

Big deal, you might be thinking. I don't spend *that* much time looking for things like that. No? If you spend just one hour a week looking for hard-to-find information, at your going rate of $350 an hour, you're losing $18,200 a year. Holy cow! (If you're thinking, *Gee, I don't make that much an your, so I guess it doesn't matter if I waste time,* then you are in even deeper trouble because you will have a lot of difficulty making the leap to a higher hourly rate if you can't get more efficient.)

And that's not all. Not only are you wasting time, but you may be missing opportunities. Some people assume that if they take the time to create and maintain systems, then they are wasting precious time they might better spend finding new business opportunities. Not so. Opportunistic thinking is not the opposite of systems thinking, it's the same thing. If you have the right systems in place, you'll be freer to be opportunistic. So, not only could you be losing $18, 200 a year without systems (at a very minimum), but you could be missing opportunities for additional revenue sources.

Now that I have your attention, let's have a look at the important systems in your business. Every business is a system, containing many subsystems. Remember our autonomic nervous system? A healthy business runs just as smoothly, with subsystems integrated into one healthy system. When one part of the system breaks down, it necessarily affects the rest of the system. The money is in the system, not just in the business idea or even in the competency of the service. The success of any business will ultimately be determined by the strength of the subsystems. At a minimum, subsystems should include marketing, accounting, customer service, and human resources. The better each system is, the better all systems are, because they are all interconnected.

In this chapter, we look at how to approach building your own standardized systems. We focus on how to introduce new subsystems into your business. It's a balancing process, much like introducing a new vitamin, a new diet, or a new medicine into your body. At first there may be some adverse side effects, but once the medicine—or in our case, the subsystem—integrates with the rest of the organism, a new and better equilibrium is achieved. The only way to know whether your systems work is by testing them. I will help you create a specific plan that will include an evaluation of your current systems—what is working, what needs to be improved. Then I'll guide you through the process of creating new systems and introducing each new subsystem into the larger organism, your business. You may have growing pains, both internally and externally, as you learn how to deal with each new system, but it's worth it.

You may instinctively shy away from the notion of systems because it sounds dry. *My business isn't a factory; I'm not going to mechanize it.* Beth Schneider, president of ProcessProdigy.com, an expert in small business systems, says, "The interesting thing about systems is that there's the classic engineering piece of it. And then there's the creative side of it where you ask yourself, *How could I play this differently, to make it more colorful, more fun, more this, or more that?*"

A system should be an "elegant solution," the kind that Matthew May and Kevin Roberts refer to in their book, *The Elegant Solution: Toyota's Formula for Mastering Innovation*, one that uses the least effort to accomplish the best result. You may also have heard other variations of this principle expressed as Occam's razor (after the fourteenth-century Franciscan friar, William of Ockham) or as the law of parsimony, that all things being equal, the simplest solution tends to be the best one. Systems do not need to be and should not be complicated, and they sure shouldn't complicate your life.

When to Build a System

When is the best time to build a system? Now. Just because you are a small-business owner does not mean your business is too young for systems. The earlier you put your systems in place the better. In fact, one problem faced by many small-business owners is that they have created systems (of a sort) for their activities, but the systems are executed by the small-business owner and known only to him or her or they are all in the owner's head. That's not a system that will help you grow or even sustain your business. You can't take your eyes off the business for a moment if you're the only one who knows what's going on.

Maybe you think you have a good reason for keeping your systems in your head. In fact, there are three very common dynamics that may be at work:

1. My system is too complicated for me to explain it to other people or to write it down.
2. I couldn't trust anyone else to do it better than I do.
3. I've had systems, and they've been a waste of time; I don't want to spend time fixing them or developing new systems.

Let's look at each of these dynamics in turn.

Saying that something is too complicated to explain is a terrible excuse. If you can't describe what you're doing as a process, then you don't know what you're doing. Really. This point is so important I'm going to say it again. If you can't document what you're doing so it's understandable (i.e., apparent) for other people, then you don't know what you're doing. A system needs to be *apparent and documented* to be effective, even if you are the only one using it.

Don't trust others to do something as well as you? If you are still feeling that way, then might I suggest that you go back to the beginning of the book and start over. You will not be able to build a bigger, better business until you are willing and able to collaborate with all sorts of different people on the projects you need to get done working *on* your business, *in* your business, and *on yourself*. If people can't execute something as well as you do, perhaps the fault lies in a badly explained or inefficient system. Fortunately, once you've worked through this chapter, you'll have great systems in place.

Maybe you think, *Systems are a waste of time.* Yes, it takes time to develop systems while you're building your business. You might feel like you are wasting time, even missing the few opportunities that come your way in the early days. You're not. I guarantee you that if you take a systems-based approach to building your business, difficult as it may be at the beginning when you don't yet have much of a business, you will end up with a bigger, better business and more opportunities worth pursuing in the end.

Another reason that so many people avoid documenting their systems is because it can seem to be overwhelming (in addition to being a waste of time). Where do you even start? I resisted it myself for a while, especially because I love to move quickly. It's one of my strengths—being able to get more done in a single day than most people do all week. I was concerned that by putting everything into a process and document-ing it, I might have to follow the "rules" and rules would slow me down. Plus, I don't like to follow rules that are just unnecessary policy constraints. That just seems boring to me. Many of us like to wing it. We make it up as we go along, sort of like the Cartesian, step-by-step approach to doing things that we discussed earlier, rather than a systems approach or scenario planning. "Winging it" is not the same thing as learning in action. But you know that by now. (Don't you?) Not only is winging it unsustainable over the long term, but when you take that kind of approach, it is hard to bring other people into your business, or to outsource, or, in fact, to leverage yourself in any way.

Here's yet another way to think about the time spent following a system versus a systemless approach. When you go to bed at night, do you put the clothes you were wearing away in the closet, or in a drawer or in the laundry hamper, or do you jumble them on the floor of your closet, thinking that you just want to get into bed and not miss the opportunity of two more minutes of sleep? By the end of the week, there's five days, worth of clothing jumbled on the floor, you can't find what you want to wear, and it takes you an hour to clean up your closet and put things where they belong. So for two extra minutes of sleep per night (a total of 10 minutes of sleep), you caused an hour of extra work for yourself. Not only that, chances are that you spent some extra time in the morning trying to find something to wear that got lost at the bottom of the pile. You could have caught that extra two minutes of sleep and more if you didn't have to wake up early to find your clothes, if only you had a system in place of putting your clothes away at night. You also could have avoided all that stress. Maybe you are a neat person, but I'm guessing there's something else, many things else, analogous to this happening in your business.

Figure 10.1 shows what life might look like if you try to do it yourself and keep it all in your head.

Figure 10.1 Overwhelmed

Convinced? In case not, let's take what may seem like a step backward for a moment into what you could call systems theory—what's it all about? There are two questions I want to answer: First, what's a system? And second, what's a system in the context of a small-business owner (specifically for someone who wants to go from being booked solid to beyond booked solid, to relieve or remove unwanted constraints and put productive constraints in place)?

The term *system* can be ambiguous. It's used in different forms and contexts that may or may not be accurate as it relates to going beyond booked solid. Beth Schneider describes a small-business system as "how you do the work of your business": how you plan, how you work with your clients, how you follow up with new prospective clients. It's the specific steps that support what you're doing. It's what you're doing minute by minute, hour by hour, day by day, month by month, year by year in your business. Interestingly enough, you have already created many systems in your business, either intentionally or just by the act of working in your business. The only thing is—the systems you have set up may not be the most productive or effective. They may not allow you to grow and may only exist in your head, which means you are the only one who can execute the system.

You need to learn how to think in systems: How do I want the phone answered? How do I want customers to be treated when they walk in the door? How do I want customer invoices handled? How do I want changes made to the web site? What fonts do I want used on all external administrative and marketing documents? How am I going to manage all the usernames and passwords for all the online accounts? It's a way of thinking: *Here's what we're going to do. Now, how are we going to do it?*

When you start a one-person product or service-based business, you need to create awareness of what you're selling in order to get clients. Seventy-five percent of your time is often spent on marketing. The other 25 percent of your time is spent on working in your business—serving your clients or customers and dealing with the administrative details that accompany that work. The reason that most people don't start thinking about systems or process in the early stages is because they can get away with not thinking about it or doing anything about it. It's natural that we place our attention on what is most pressing, most urgent. And when you don't have enough clients to pay the bills, then, of course, your most pressing issue is getting clients.

That's why I wrote *Book Yourself Solid* first. Marketing is often the first big thing you need to master. However, you get to a point in your business where the work is pretty consistent and the scales are tipped to where you feel like 75 percent of what you're doing is dealing with administrative and operational crap (did I just say crap?) that you don't like doing or simply shouldn't be doing because it's a totally unproductive use of your time and is preventing you from focusing on the important work of continuing to grow your business.

Wouldn't it be ideal to start building systems into your business at an earlier stage, maybe from day one? Beth Schneider believes that how you run your business is just as important as how you market your business. I second that. As she points out, you may market like a rock star and have truckloads of clients or customers running to you for service, but if you can't fulfill the work or serve them, then what's the point? But if you didn't start this process yet, no problem. There is still time for the cure.

Building Systems

We've agreed you need systems as early as possible, systems that are visible and documented. Let's start. "Umm, hold on a minute," you're saying. I know. I know. Starting is the big hurdle. People get hung up before they even start. I've experienced this myself. It feels like there are so many things that you have to do, that it's almost mind-boggling to try to articulate the list, let alone document everything that you do. It's a massive project, and you're booked solid. You barely have time to brush your teeth. It's unrealistic to spend the hours and hours needed to first identify everything that you are currently doing to run your business and then document it all and then, on top of that, to work on improving each and every process.

You must do it. You can do it. There is no choice in the matter. You can do it yourself. You can have your team do it. You can hire someone like Beth to help you (or even do it for you). That's how I started. But, whatever way you choose, this must be done if you want to go beyond booked solid. There is no alternative to systematizing your business. There is no alternative to eliminating waste in your business and life. Simply put: If you don't do this, you don't move on.

Let's jump right in by getting specific about where you need systems. There are six major systems categories in just about every business:

1. Financial systems
2. Administrative systems
3. Communication systems
4. Sales systems
5. Marketing systems
6. Client support systems

Creating apparent, documented systems in each of these categories is essential for you to:

- Stay competitive
- Improve productivity
- Cut costs
- Improve customer service
- Improve quality
- Reduce time to market
- Reduce inventories
- Better manage cash flow
- Plan and allocate resources
- Respond to customers changing needs

It's been true in the earlier chapters, and it is true again with systems. This is an iterative process. A system is not forever. It is for as long as the particular system continues to provide the elegant solution. Over time, businesses grow and change. Their systems may no longer meet the information-processing requirements of the business. The current systems must be improved either by making changes to the existing systems or by replacing what exists with new systems.

If you are reading this book, you are likely embarking on some major changes in your business. You're extending your existing business architecture, or you're building a whole new architecture. You will need to reorganize the way your company operates, and you will need new, dynamic systems to support the changes. Not only that, you will need to be able to quickly implement new business processes and their supporting technology.

Systems can help you build something bigger that you still run but don't have to work so hard in any more. At a minimum, systems will help you stop doing the stuff you don't like and get back just to serving clients, doing the work you love.

When creating systems or processes, it's important to base every process in your business on a desired outcome and to measure the success of the process. Otherwise you have no idea if your systems are creating positive or negative constraints in your business. Remember when we talked about constraints? Well, systems are one form of constraint. A system can be a positive constraint if it's working to serve you and the objectives of your business. Or it can be a negative constraint if it's not serving your goals—if it's not a productive process and leads to waste. We need to create lean systems (aka elegant solutions), to think lean, to be lean with the goal of eliminating waste. That's what good systems ultimately do.

Beth Schneider suggests the following process for creating systems in the small business:

- Document what you're currently doing in your business.
- Now that you have your standard procedures documented, set a desired outcome for each business process.
- Improve on the current processes.

Not so complicated, is it? Let's keep moving. We've got the momentum.

Identify What You're Doing in Your Business

Start by focusing on what's happening in your business. What's happening on a daily, weekly, monthly, yearly basis?

- Are you writing copy?
- Are you following up with clients?
- Are you going to events?
- Are you networking?
- Are you answering e-mail?
- Are you answering sales calls?
- Are you processing new clients?
- Are you fulfilling products?
- Are you sending invoices?
- Are you collecting payments from declined credit cards?
- Are you creating holiday greeting cards?

What are you doing? And, most importantly, *how* are you doing all of this?

Beth recommends starting with a brainstorm about what you think you do. Then she likes to have her clients keep a log for one week. What you think you do is probably not quite the same as what you actually do. It's kind of like those food diaries that people on diets keep. It can truly be shocking to discover what you really eat every day versus what you thought you ate. No less surprising is the difference between what you think you do and what you actually do. Let's figure it out.

Once you have this record, divide the information up into the different categories of your business as we listed earlier in the chapter.

> ### Exercise
>
> Keep a small pad of paper and a pen on your desk or with you every moment for a week. Record everything (and I mean everything) you do during the day and how long it took. Looked at my calendar. Looked for someone's phone number (how?— piece of paper, address book, online yellow pages). Made a call. Wrote a letter. Reviewed financials. Looked at pet tricks on YouTube.com. Cleaned bike wheels. Discussed operating issues with assistant. And so on.

These are your Standard Work Sheets, detailing what work needs to be done in each area of the business. You might want to narrow the exercise at first by being specific about what you're going to focus on documenting. Choose one category to hone in on at first. Michael Gerber, author of *The E-Myth books*, suggests a simple model: Look at your lead generation. Look at your lead conversion. And look at your product delivery.

Whether you start with one area or as many as you can, here's a partial list of the sorts of things you may want to tackle:

Lead Generation

- Online
  - Search engine optimization
  - E-mail promotions and e-newsletters
  - Web site opt-in forms and autoresponder e-mail campaigns
  - Google ad words
  - And more . . .
- Mailing
  - Greeting card design
  - Database management (contact entries and updates)

  - Greeting card messages
  - Card promotional schedules (when do they get sent out?)
  - How is the postage paid?
  - What is the follow-up?
  - And more . . .

You get the point. You're going to want to do this for every part of the business.

Document Your Current Processes

From a lean perspective, the first thing you should do in approaching any process is to map or document the value stream, following the actual path of material or paper or information through your processes. It's best to actually walk the path to get the full experience. Do it. Don't just think it.

Once you have your Standard Work Sheets generated from your daily log exercise, you can begin to create Standard Workflow Charts, or Standard Process Maps (same thing). These are charts that literally document how work flows in your business (Figure 10.2). When X happens, then Y, or Z, or A. If a customer responds in this way, do that. If a customer responds in that way, do this. The object is to account for every possible workflow scenario in your business. A workflow chart, or process map, should be created following a very specific format so you can detail (and ultimately improve) workflow and execution.

Inherent in the word *standard* (as in standard process) should be a level of *quality*. Your standard process map should represent the current best workflow. Then improve it by working toward the ideal to which you've been striving but have perhaps not quite achieved—yet. In this way, quality is built into the standard, and you have already begun the cycle of improvement. You will be constantly striving to improve your standard processes, to raise the bar and to improve quality. There is

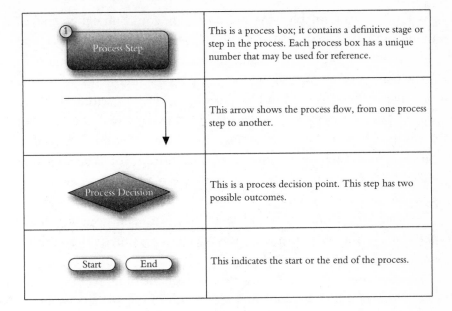

(1) Process Step	This is a process box; it contains a definitive stage or step in the process. Each process box has a unique number that may be used for reference.
↓	This arrow shows the process flow, from one process step to another.
Process Decision	This is a process decision point. This step has two possible outcomes.
Start End	This indicates the start or the end of the process.

Figure 10.2   Standard Elements of a Process Map

no "end." But don't be discouraged. Once you've created a process to improve your processes, the ongoing improvement will be practically automatic.

By developing standard processes, everything will flow more smoothly. Haphazard is not a process and will lead to breakdown and likely to client dissatisfaction. For example, I'm putting new hardwood floors in my house. Into the project, the hardwood floor people told me that they "don't do open stairs, because they don't deal with spindles." Oh. Would have been nice to know at the beginning; and had they had a process, they probably would have told me earlier. But now I need a stair contractor to be coordinated with the floor people. So, okay, I call the stair people. They come right away, but then they don't deliver the estimate when they said they would (no process or had a process but didn't follow it). I'm starting to assume they will be even worse once they have my money (i.e., will they show up this year?).

Process was notably absent from both companies. I wasn't so much upset at the time it took to deliver the estimate. It was that they promised the estimate quickly and didn't deliver. Remember what Flores said about making and fulfilling commitments. Well, process helps you make and fulfill your obligations to customers. There should have been a process that identified if stairs would be part of the project and let the customer (me) know early that there needed to be a second contractor and how the coordination would occur (don't leave that solution to the customer). How long it takes to deliver an estimate to a client should be a process, too. And so on. My contractors haven't read this book, and so I'll stay calm and hope for floors and stairs in the proper order, on budget and on time (although that seems unlikely given the lack of process).

Kody Bateman at SendOutCards.com, on the other hand, has processes for everything. In customer service, for example, there's a documented a-b-c process that every new customer service rep gets when he or she starts. There's a step-by-step system to learn and a "mini-baptism by fire" on the job. But the result of all Kody's documentation and visibility is that every customer service rep hits the ground running and is fully up to speed by the end of week two, delivering the same consistently high customer service as others in the process.

Set a Desired Outcome for Each Business Function

Once you've determined what you're currently doing, you want to set a desired outcome for each one of the processes. Just because you have a process in your business doesn't mean you're achieving the desired result. A process should be designed to create harmony and balance in your business. As you are building systems, you need to ask yourself, what is the value of this process to the customer (who might be you)? I wasn't so much upset because the contractor didn't get me the estimate quickly enough. It was that he said one thing and did another. What's the process? How long does it take? Speed of response may not be paramount. Designing a system that responds quickly may have no value to the customer and may overwhelm the system. Know the value of each potential outcome as you are designing the system.

Ask yourself at every step: What is the value to the customer? Every time there's waste (value lost) in the process, it's like a rock in a stream. The water has to flow around it, sideways, in the wrong direction. That means wasted effort. The less flow you have in a process, the more inefficiencies and waste are hidden. You and your team will just assume that processes take days or weeks or months to complete or that they cost X dollars. A typical help desk, for example, might have one person managing the workload. That person in turn distributes tickets to other people, who are tasked with responding to the inquiry. And those people in turn may need to get information from someone else entirely. Because the system is so dispersed, it doesn't flow well. It stops and starts as people are waiting for information or for someone else to complete a task. But no one can really see where the waste is because no one sees the whole process; it's too dispersed. The problems are buried instead of rising to the surface, as they would if the process flowed. Maybe it can all be done more efficiently—more quickly and/or at lower cost.

You can't determine the added value of any one individual in your business without looking at the actual process in which he or she is working as it relates to the final outcome. What you may find is that you and the people you work with are churning out tons of information or doing many activities, but that very little actual work is adding value to the outcome. The clearer you are about what adds value, the easier it will be to reduce waste.

If, for example, my stair contractor had a process that dictated that they respond to every customer with a quote within 24 hours, the result would probably be an imbalance in the workload. While there is some value to the customer in the 24-hour response time, the increment in value over, say, a 72-hour response time is probably not enough to compensate for the imbalance created inside the company, scrambling to respond. Toyota does not build a totally custom car for any customer because it creates too irregular a workflow. To stay lean, elegant, and parsimonious means understanding the value of every outcome and ironing out imbalances inside and outside. Toyota will build the car you order, and they give you lots of options in the ordering.

One of the big wastes in the service business is waiting for information or information waiting for someone else. A fast response time may just mean that information spends more time in the client's inbox. No value there, so why do it?

Part of creating a process means asking the right questions, the questions that identify why a business function exists and what the desired outcome is. David Allen, author of *Getting Things Done: The Art of Stress-Free Productivity*, has created what he calls the GTD (getting things done, of course) system. The crux of his system is engaging people to ask themselves the right questions, all the time. "What is my vision?" "What are my short-term goals?" Instead of asking, "How much am I making?" ask, "How much waste am I producing and how can I reduce it?" Asking the right questions is the key to creating an effective process. Look at your current outcomes and analyze their value. Squeeze waste out of the process and the outcome.

Improve on the Current Process

Once you've set a desired outcome, you need to measure the success of that outcome. You'll do that by measuring what you're doing (the expenditure of resources) against the result you're getting (the value). From there the work is to simplify the process until you're getting more of what you want with less effort and cost—that's lean, elegant, and parsimonious.

Then once you have your new standardized processes, you'll find that problems are brought to the surface naturally. Once they are visible, you can go to work on solving the problems immediately, continuing the cycle of improvement. Improve on the current process, and then continue improving on the process.

In order to improve the process, follow the lean method for keeping it simple:

- Look at what's going on. I mean actually, physically, have a look at what the problem is. Don't just take someone else's word for it.
- Analyze the situation with others. Don't rush to a solution on your own. Let others weigh in, so you can get a more complete picture.
- Ask "why" five times. To get at the root cause of any problem, you need to ask and keep asking why you're having this problem. The first answer to the question is rarely right. Ask the question five times, and see what comes up.
- Before solving a problem, stop, reflect on, and consider all options.

One of the biggest benefits of this message is that it will help you not to blame others, or to be defensive, when something goes wrong—the typical knee-jerk reaction. And, yes, I've been guilty of leaping to conclusions and blaming people many times myself. I'm trying to do better.

You improve your processes by eliminating waste. Only add steps to the process if they add value to the outcome, which means keeping in mind "who" the customer for the outcome is, whether they are internal (you or someone else on your team) or external (customer, vendor, or partner). Examine your process from the customer's perspective. In the case of Michael's Event Booking Process (Figure 10.3), the person or organization hiring me is the customer. In the case of Michael's Event Management Process (Figure 10.4), I am the customer. It's me who is being served by the event management process. It's my schedule that's being organized in the best possible way, to suit my needs (to ensure, for example, that I'm not traveling too much or too little). The first question to ask to start examining the effectiveness of the process is, "What does the customer want from this process?"

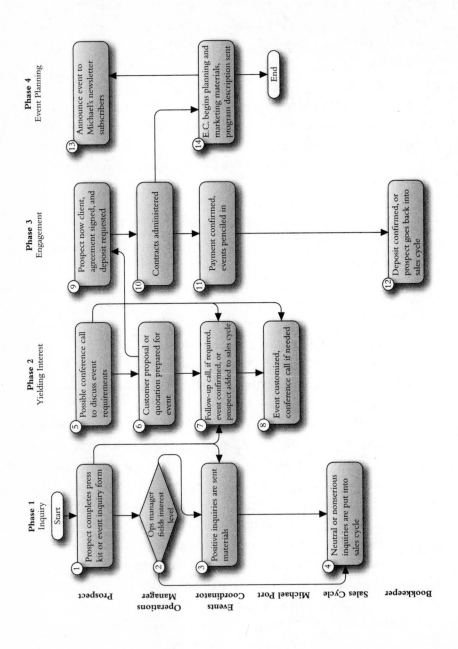

1. Prospect completes press kit or event inquiry form online.

2. Ops Manager checks availability in Michael's calendar. Then follows up with phone call or e-mail to determine prospect's level of interest.

3. Positive inquiries are sent press kit and book via e-mail.

4. Neutral or nonserious inquiries are put into sales cycle.

5. If needed, Michael and Ops Manager have conference call with prospect to discuss event requirements.

6. Ops Manager prepares proposal/quotation for event customized to serve prospect's needs.

7. If confirmation from prospect has not been received, Events Coordinator follows up to 10 days after press kit mailed out. If prospect is still interested, Event Coordinator confirms go-ahead to Ops Manager. If response is negative, prospect goes into sales cycle.

8. Michael provides his feedback for customization of event. May have a teleconference to discuss needs and requirements.

9. Prospect becomes client. Accepts, signs, and returns agreement and sends deposit.

10. Ops Manager requests deposit and sends copy of agreement to Events Coordinator. Ops Manager prints agreement, adds to agreement binder, and creates client file. Assigns contract number, and adds to tracking spreadsheet.

11. Event Coordinator confirms if payment is received from bookkeeper. If so, puts hold on dates in Michael's calendar.

12. Bookkeeper confirms deposit is received. If deposit is not received, prospect goes back into sales cycle.

13. If event is open to the public, announce via e-mail to Michael's newsletter subscribers.

14. Events Coordinator begins planning and coordination process. As per the contract, sends client marketing materials and program description.

Figure 10.3 Michael's Event Booking Process

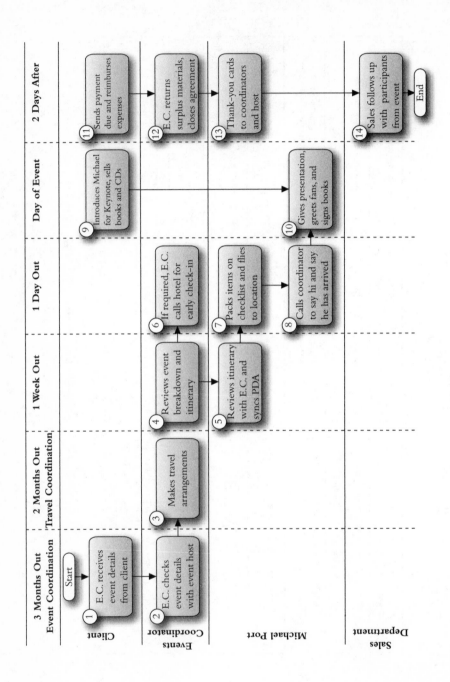

(1)	Client sends Events Coordinator:
	  * event time line and breakdown
	  * on-site contacts and event address
	  * sponsor hotel address
	  * number of attendees
	  * AV requirements
		(8)	Michael calls coordinator to say "hi" and that he has arrived.

(2)	Events Coordinator communicates with client about:
	  * transaction processing for sale of books and CDs
	  * order form printing, banner, and handout setup
	  * Shipment of books/CDs to event location
	  * Sound and video needs
	
	Events Coordinator invites volunteers to assist.
		(9)	Events Coordinator introduces Michael for keynote. Sells books, and CDs.

(3)	Contact Amex platinum travel services to book travel arrangements:
	  * direct flight and hotel
	  * ensure frequent flier miles are used
	  * nonsmoking room
	  * wireless access
	  * prepare Michael's itinerary and trip planner
	  * arrange for car rental/vehicle pickup
	  * put details in Michael's calendar for synchronizing with PDA
		(10)	Michael presents/facilitates. Greets fans, does book signing.

(4)	Review event breakdown and travel itinerary with Michael. Ensure he has packed everything required. Set up Michael's out-of-office e-mail message.	(11)	Client sends remaining payment and reimburses travel and incidentals.
(5)	Michael reviews itinerary with Events Coordinator one week prior to event, syncs PDA.	(12)	Events Coordinator has extra books, CDs, banners shipped back to wharehouse, closes out agreement.
(6)	If early check-in is required, Events Coordinator calls hotel to request.	(13)	Michael sends thank-you cards to coordinators and hosts for their efforts and hospitality.
(7)	Michael packs clothes and accessories as indicated on packing checklist and flies to location.	(14)	Sales follows up on further interest with participants from event.

Figure 10.4 Michael's Event Management Process

In each process, my administrators perform many separate tasks, but generally only a small number of these tasks add value, as far as the customer is concerned. Of course, some of the nonvalue steps are necessary to a process but don't directly add value for the customer. The point is to minimize the time spent on nonvalue-added tasks.

Jeffrey K. Liker, author of *The Toyota Way*, says that Toyota identified seven primary types of nonvalue-adding waste in its business: overproduction, motion (of operator or machine), waiting (of operator or machine), conveyance, processing itself, inventory (raw material), and correction (rework and scrap). Liker included an eighth waste (a personal favorite)—untapped employee creativity.

I have adapted Toyota and Liker's lists for our purposes—so that they relate, not to a manufacturing process, but to a service business:

- *Overstaffing:* Hiring people for whom there is not enough work
- *Overproduction:* Producing items (work) for which there are no clients or orders
- *Waiting:* For information, resources, supplies, anything that slows down flow and creates waste
- *Overprocessing or incorrect processing:* Activity, conversations, or processes that are not necessary or are incorrectly executed
- *Unused employee creativity:* Not enlisting and empowering your team, both intellectually and emotionally, in a continuous process of improvement

In manufacturing, it's often argued that overproduction is the greatest of all waste, since it causes most of the other wastes. I think the same could hold true for a service-based business: not only overproduction of your services, but doing too much of everything that is not valuable to the internal or external customer. Overproduction waste, as Liker points out, "leads to other suboptimal behavior, like reducing your motivation to continuously improve your operations."

Earlier, I mentioned Hal's Two Great Wastes™: not speaking or not listening. It turns out that there are a lot of Less-Than-Great Wastes, too. Wastes will have different priorities, depending on the business. It's up to you to identify what the big wastes are to you and your business. The list I've given you should help in the identification process.

Typical business processes might be 90 percent waste and only 10 percent value-added work. Think back to that $18,000 you wasted looking for phone numbers. That was just the tip of the iceberg. The objective is to create continuous flow in information processes and service processes. No one produces anything before it is needed by the next person or for the next step in the process. Nothing should ever sit around waiting, except maybe things like cash savings in the bank for security and protection. Shortening the elapsed time from start of process to finished good or service will lead to best quality, lowest cost, and shortest delivery time. There are at least two customers in this process—you and your paying customers at the other end of the process. Ensuring the best-quality service benefits your paying customers, and it's also the best marketing. Ensuring the lowest cost benefits you as customer. Achieving the shortest delivery time might serve both you and your paying customer. But it might not. What's the value of each of these objectives, and where is it being created? You might not have the best service, lowest cost, *and* shortest delivery time. You might, however, find the optimal balance between the three. That's the objective of all your processes.

Getting It Right the First Time—and Fixing Problems as They Occur

Developing systems won't happen overnight. Yes, you're in a hurry. Now that you know you need them, you want them now. If possible, take the time to get your processes right the first time. Here are three steps that should help you do that:

1. Identify who the customer is for the process and the value that they need to receive.

2. Separate out the repetitive process from the one-of-a-kind process, and standardize the repetitive processes.
3. Standardize how much and what kind of one-of-a-kind tasks you will (and won't) do for the customer.

Getting it right the first time doesn't mean getting hung up on perfection. Remember the concept of satisficing? The idea here is to set a first (good enough) standard from which you can then up the standard. Yes, that seems to be contradictory. I said you might have to hold seemingly contradictory thoughts in your head at the same time. Really though, they are not. Toyota (big surprise) is a company known for its slow pace of decision making. It is a reflective company. For the Toyota Prius, the company started with 80 complete hybrid engine designs. They narrowed to 10 and then to 4 and finally to the Prius engine that's on the road today. Yet, they designed and manufactured the car in less than two years. Why? Because Toyota takes its time to get it right but once the decision is made, the change and implementation are immediate. This is how I want you to go about developing your new processes. And, for that matter, this is how you should be thinking about which business building blocks to incorporate into your new business architecture.

Try out many scenarios (processes) on paper. Figure out which one is best by testing them in real time. Once you find the best, implement immediately. That's getting it right the first time. Will it be perfect? No. Nothing ever is (yes, that old tune again). It will be the best there is for that moment. Now you've set the quality standard against which you will measure new process ideas as they arise. If they raise the standard, incorporate. If they are neutral or lower the standard, don't incorporate. Get it right the first time, and then practice *kaizen*—continuous improvement.

How did that feel? Congratulations, you've just overcome the single biggest hurdle to implementing systems—starting. If you did the exercise, then you've already started to build your systems. What's next? Keep going.

Exercise

Here's a way to practice continuous improvement. Gather your team (which might be you and your favorite teddy bear), and follow these steps to improve a particular process:

Step 1: Identify the customer and the scope of the business process. What is the value added to the customer? Is there a measurable objective? Keep in mind that you may have more than one customer on a process (internal and external).

Step 2: Determine your current state—the standard process and workflow, along with what value is being added and what is wasteful.

Step 3: Identify what your future state ought to look like—eliminate waste, identify what nonvalue-added items need to stay and how to increase value-added.

Step 4: Create a plan for implementation—What? When? Who? How will others be trained? How will you communicate?

Step 5: Get out there and do it.

Step 6: Measure your improvement—establish metrics for the improvement process, track process, build in continuous improvement. What do you measure? Lead times, delivery, quality, and productivity.

11

How To—
Hire Others,
Outsource, and
Leverage Yourself

The efficiency of most workers is beyond the control of the management and depends more than has been supposed upon the willingness of men to do their best.

—Sumner H. Slichter

Systems, of course, aren't the only way you can leverage yourself more and work less. Outsourcing and hiring other people is another. But again, you aren't (and shouldn't) abdicate your responsibilities to others. You've probably heard people talk about abdication versus delegation. Certainly, delegation is a better approach, but I'd go one step further. I don't think you should delegate either (not to people or to systems). Even delegation implies that we stop paying attention because we have passed off one of our responsibilities. It may also mean that you stop looking at what's going on in your business. That's not so good. You can't manage or improve what you can't see.

It's like having piles of things to do on your desk. If you're like most people, what's on the bottom is least likely to get done because you can't see it. Not only that, you may not even know it needs to get done because you can't see what's below the top of the pile, and that item slips from your priority list and then from your memory. In an early effort to get organized, I started filing things. It was all well and good, except that my files were disappearing out of sight into a file drawer. Out of sight, out of mind. The urgency of a task that had gotten filed was lost. Now I work with an open filing system, one of those rolling file storage units, that allows me to simultaneously keep everything organized and see it at the same time.

Delegating is often the same thing as filing something away in a closed drawer. It feels organized, but you've stopped looking. This chapter is not about abdication or delegation; it's about collaboration with people to share work—so that you leverage your time better and ultimately work less.

You can do much more with others than you can do alone. If you're like a lot of business owners, you might find yourself overwhelmed and unable to find ways to bring in more profits without simply putting in more time and effort doing the same old things. Or maybe you're eager to create strategic alliances but just can't figure out the steps to take that will really work to expand your income. Imagine what it would be like if you had your own team of professionals working to help grow your business and create new streams of prospects and income that would basically run on autopilot. It's simpler than you think. Collaboration is everything involving other people—from hiring, to outsourcing, to partnering in strategic alliances. Remember, I said "collaboration"—not abdication or even delegation. And once you've discovered how to put your business into the "collaboration mindset"—whether it's in product creation, event hosting, cross-promotion, or any other strategy—you will immediately take your business and your bottom line to the next level.

Hiring

One of the biggest mistakes a small business can make (any business, really) is finding people with the right skills (seems great) but the wrong attitude. You can't change people. They are who they are. And what people know is often less important than who they are. The best predictor of behavior is past behavior. You may think that you have changed over the years. Isn't that what therapy or yoga or medita-tion is all about? (I'm not knocking any of those. I tried therapy—twice—used to teach yoga, and now meditate daily.) What things like yoga and therapy indicate is a person's openness to change. That's not the same thing as change. I'm not saying people can't improve. They can. Everyone has the capacity to be more than one version of their "selves." You may be a happier, more relaxed person when you are pursuing your dream than when you are doing something you hate. Being a better version of you is not the same as changing. So, maybe you have changed, but probably not as much as you think.

For decades the U.S. Air Force did research on personality types. Beginning in the 1950s, researchers tracked their subjects by observing their behavior and interviewing their families, friends, and colleagues. The conclusion? Basic personality traits did not change. Attitude is often one of the most basic personality traits. Don't hire someone thinking you can cheer them up or motivate them or inspire them to become a happier or more positive (and, therefore, more effective) employee. Just because they have a Harvard MBA, were a Rhodes scholar, and worked with the Peace Corps in the deepest jungle some-where may not mean they have the right attitude for their role in your business—and your life.

You need to create systems for finding the best people. Aha, so systems come first. Well, not exactly, because you need a good person, or people, to create the system. More on this dilemma later.

Ann Rhoades is largely credited for creating the early Southwest Airlines hiring methodology and is something of a legend in human resources circles. In a *Fast Company* article in August 1996, "Hire for Attitude, Train for Skill," she describes asking this signature question of potential new hires: "Tell me about the last time you broke the rules." A long silence or a noncommittal response is an indication that a candidate is trying to figure out what she wants to hear. "The good ones," she says, "don't care."

Rhoades' question got me thinking about when and how I break rules. I'm a bit of a rules guy. I used to think I wanted to work for the FBI and track down bad guys who broke rules, until I realized that the FBI had too many rules. You're thinking, "So what kind of rules does he break?" Here's one example: People in my field like to say, "Always sell from the stage." In other words, never give a talk without pitching specific items you're selling. It's one of the "rules" for selling in my field. I don't do it, at least not the way it's commonly done. But people still run up to me after my talks and ask me how they can work with me. Another thing people say in my field is that you must have a 100 percent money-back guarantee on all your programs and seminars, and other stuff. . . . I don't. I believe that I am delivering a good service, and if the person who signs up doesn't do the work, I'm not giving them back their money. Money-back guarantees are not a sales tactic I use for high-value services. Sure, if I'm offering a $30 booklet, you can have a money-back guarantee. But if you are signing up for a seminar, for example, I'm making a commitment to my customers to deliver a great service and they make a commitment to stick with it.

Interestingly, I learned that there's a great reason to do things my way. Barry Schwartz, in *The Paradox of Choice,* describes an experiment where two groups of people were sold two identical fans—identical in every way except that one of the groups was sold fans that had a lifetime money-back guarantee and the other group's fans did not. Guess which group of people was ultimately more satisfied? That's right. Those who bought the fans knowing that "all sales are final" were happier. Why? They made a bigger psychological commitment to the fan when they bought it. The other group, who had the lifetime money-back guarantee, continued to question their decision, second-guessing their choice. The bottom line is that those who make nonreversible commitments are more likely to be satisfied with their choice. I broke the money-back rule in my business, but it turns out I may end up with more satisfied customers and, ultimately, more profits. And, as an aside, I'm not as tough as I sound. Up to 48 hours before a seminar or program begins, a person can get a full refund. Not only that, if someone gets gravely ill during our work together or has some other real crisis, a serious business reversal, for example, I break my own rule and give his or her money back. So . . . I break my own rules, too, except for the number-one rule of taking care of others. What I want you to notice is how there is a specific and thoughtful process behind each of these choices. It's not haphazard.

Ann Rhoades' question about rule breaking is part of her system for identifying a particular type of person. Map out in advance the personality traits and attitude you need in the person you're hiring. Design interview questions that will draw out this aspect of a person's character. I'd go much further though. Create a matrix for success "on the job" for the particular position you're hiring. For example, practical learning, teamwork, tolerance for stress, communication, attention to detail, adaptability/flexibility, and motivation may all be traits (not just skills) that you need in the job. Hire around those matrix traits.

The best way to evaluate people is to watch them work. Some companies take this literally. BMW has a simulated assembly line. Job candidates get 90 minutes to perform a variety of work-related tasks. Toyota and Subaru do something similar. If you're hiring for contract work, you can do the same. Give a small assignment or project with very specific details, and watch your potential new hire work. See how they deal with the critical issues that make up your matrix. In fact, you can even work in the kinds of obstacles and issues that come up in your business. If flexibility is a big part of your culture, start them on a project and call them the next day with changes or additions to the project. See how they handle it. If they are going to do customer service for you, ask some real customers to give them a hard time and see how they handle it. Companies that hire smart often start their recruiting close to home—promoting their own employees and drawing from their pool of contractors. That way they already know how a person works and what personality traits are going to show up on the job.

I once hired an assistant who had all the right skills—tech savvy, bright, experienced, and so on. But he didn't like to reflect on his communication style, an outgrowth of what I found to be his somewhat blind and arrogant attitude. When I would try to speak with him about problems that others were having with him, he would point out all the tasks he had accomplished. He wasn't open to hearing about any ways in which he might change. Sure, he was doing the tasks of the job, but he was bringing down the general morale with his prickly presence. Even though he got things done, it wasn't worth it to keep him.

If you have a rigorous selection process, then ultimately you will be able to give the great people you hire the freedom they need once they're hired. Which brings us back to the balance between people and systems—once you've done the hiring; you need to create systems for managing and supporting people, so they can do the best job possible.

Ron Quintero has systematized his business as much as he can. He bases his decisions on solid business metrics. As he says, "Combining the right people with the right process and then measuring what's going on within those environments is how I'm able to make decisions that will improve the development of the business." He has, among other things, accountability spreadsheets, project sheets, and goal sheets for each department. If a breakdown happens, he looks at the spreadsheets to track its source. Not so he can single someone out, but for the opposite reason—so he can focus on the breakdown itself, instead of pinpointing a particular person to take the blame. As you can imagine, his team has a great attitude.

Outsourcing

Outsourcing is about developing long-term and project-by-project relationships with professionals who have expertise outside your own. It may come in the form of placing the reins of a particular project in someone else's hands, or it may take the form of a more strategic alliance of shared work. Either way, the effect is the same—to outsource work that would normally be done inside the company.

According to a survey by Forrester of companies and organizations buying outsourcing services:

- 53 percent reported that they have outsourcing challenges because their companies lack project management skills (not so for you after reading this book!).
- 58 percent reported they lack a good process for specifying the work (not so for you once again!).
- 45 percent said they did not have the right metrics for measuring performance (man, you've got everything covered now!).

Collaborating with others creates scale in your business by increasing your leverage. Why? Because to collaborate effectively you need to:

- Isolate activities that generate more income than they cost to have others do.
- Identify where to place your energy and focus according to what you are pursuing and what you love.
- Stay tightly focused on the core activities.

Collaborating with others also creates range by bringing together different talents and perspectives. This is particularly important if you are adding services or serving new clients. Your talents alone are probably not sufficient for that new business.

Here are some key points to keep in mind when searching for a company or an individual to provide you with outsourcing solutions:

- How will they integrate into the big picture?
- Do their values and philosophy match yours?
- What sort of staff is on hand to provide workable outsourcing solutions? Meet the team.
- What are you buying (set and manage expectations)?
- Is there a clear chain of command?
- Is there a language barrier that could be problematic?
- Does the company have a solid financial track record, and are its growth plans realistic?
- Does the company have the commitment, stability, and strength of the management team to provide you with successful outsourcing solutions?
- What sort of image and reputation does the company carry?
- Are they on the cutting edge? What is the company's track record for innovation and improvements—can they, with your involvement, build the processes you need?

It's easy to find firms that can serve your needs. Don't necessarily hire the first one you find. Remember, the best way to evaluate people is to watch them work. No matter how excited you are by the prospect of removing some of your current constraints by hiring others, take time to see how you fit together. You're hoping to build long-term relationships. Note that I've been using the word *firm* rather than person or individual to describe your outsourcing options. I think you should avoid hiring individuals who do not have any backup of their own. Without it, they can become a "single point of failure" in your business. If they go down, you go down. I got burnt over and over by this outsourcing danger in the early days, until I got tired of the pain and insecurity of too many single points of failure. I'm not an unsympathetic person, but after a while, it's an inordinate burden to be crippled in your business by one person's extended flu or time off for a personal crisis. Now I work only with firms made up of people who possess the right attitude and skills for the projects and tasks they handle. My accounting, bookkeeping, legal, administrative, and technical needs are handled by professionals from around the world, professionals who have backup built into their systems. Take this seriously—no matter what size of business you are currently running. Be willing to pay extra for it. It's worth it.

If you hire individuals to work inside your office, you can still make sure you don't have any single points of failure. Ideally, each person you hire has a backup who can easily step in and assume the standard work practices; that's why you have standard work practices and systems. The backup may be a temp from a firm you trust, or it could be an in-office support group who are completely interchangeable—they are all trained in all responsibilities. If you've completely documented all functions of the business, it can be done.

Here are a few online resources for connecting with different types of professionals who can work locally or virtually. If you use these referral sites, I suggest testing only those who already have lots of positive reviews posted about them and their work:

- Elance.com: Use Elance to get work done without the overhead and hassle of traditional hiring. Post projects to the Elance professional network, and use Elance's tools to hire, manage, and pay for the work on demand. (I found Bob D'Amico, who did the illustrations for this book, on Elance.)
- iFreelance.com: Same concept as Elance.com.
- ScriptLance.com: Again, same thing.

- RentACoder.com: Find a computer programmer.
- GetAFreelancer.com: Again, find a computer programmer.

Think outside your borders, both nationally and internationally, when you're thinking about outsourcing. A *Miami Herald* article pointed out that small firms, maybe even more than big companies, are staying in business by outsourcing overseas. Of course, there's all the politics of so-called off-shoring. People worry that by sending jobs overseas, there's a net loss in U.S. jobs because people aren't hiring locally. But, in many cases, there would be no company at all if they didn't outsource some functions overseas. Local hiring may only be possible because companies are able to find lower-cost outsourcing solutions for some of their projects or administrative needs.

Wherever and whoever you outsource to, you must develop stable partnerships with your outside vendors, and they in turn must be capable, trustworthy, and willing to follow, establish, and/or develop standardized workflow and processes with you or for you. You must also be willing to continuously improve on the process to eliminate waste. Just because you've outsourced doesn't mean you stop managing. You will still need to establish metrics to measure the conditions of satisfaction, just as you do in every other area of your business. Without metrics, how could you improve workflow and working relationships? You get the picture.

Strategic Alliances and Partnerships

Strategic alliances and partnerships are another great way to leverage your talents, skills, and resources to their best use. When should you form a partnership with someone outside your business? When together you can create something better than either of you could individually. In other words, go into partnership with someone when $1 + 1 = 3$. Partnerships are not formed just because you find someone whose talents and skills are different from or complementary to yours. You can hire someone for a particular skill, or you can outsource. You only want to create a profit-sharing relationship when you can build something bigger together than you could alone. And the partnership should end when the math no longer adds up, when $1+1 = 2$ or less.

Dr. Mike Berkley has built his business on strategic alliances. Alone, it would take an enormous amount of effort and resources for Mike to develop a full-service wellness center offering all the diverse services he offers. Instead, he finds other like-minded service providers and brings them together in a profit-sharing relationship. He benefits because he gets their expertise in yoga, nutrition, homeopathy, or whatever their skill is. On the other side, the experts he brings in benefit from the luster of his established brand. It's a win-win situation.

Leverage Is Being a Leader and Getting Others to Take the Lead

You know how to outsource, and you know how to hire. You know when to create strategic alliances. Systems alone are not going to take care of the rest. To go beyond booked solid, you need to be a leader.

A leader's job is to make appropriate, decisive decisions. It sounds simple, but making a decision and sticking to it is something that many, many people have great difficulty doing. It's hard not to want to rethink a decision, and at times it is absolutely appropriate. But commitment (because after all what else is a decision?) can be intimidating. So to be a leader, you will most certainly also need to be able to manage high levels of stress (not just yours but other people's—employees, partners, family, etc.).

Not only do you need to provide leadership in your business, but you also need to nurture other leaders within the enterprise. This is how you'll leverage yourself. This is a critical step, and it's amazing how many small-business owners don't do it. (Remember working on yourself?) They justify not hiring other leadership-quality people into their business because it's not big enough or because they fear that if they nurture another leader, then that person will threaten their position or leave and compete. I suppose those things are real dangers, but when they are weighed against the benefits, the choice is obvious. Why would you want to hire someone who wasn't the best? When you hire someone as smart as or smarter than you who can grow into a leadership role, you are the ultimate beneficiary. You can earn more (because that person is helping the business grow) and work less (because they can take over some of your workload)! As for the fear of potential competition or being usurped, if you hire people with the right attitude and treat them well (the Platinum Rule), they won't want to leave; and if they do, it will be with the best of goodwill, not because they are trying to undermine your future. Enough said.

When you are looking to hire potential leaders, you need to go back to the matrix of traits we talked about a few pages ago. Initiative may be one of the most important traits you'll need to have in your matrix when you're looking for a future leader.

Besides initiative, which you have loads of or you wouldn't be booked solid or on your way, let's look at what else it takes to be a great leader. No surprise that one of the hallmarks of great leaders is that they are "in touch" with themselves and with the people who work with them. It's the best way to be a good role model. What's necessary? Clarity, honesty, integrity, openness, self-respect, and treating every individual with dignity—not once in a while to get something done or get something from someone—but all the time. Great leaders rarely, if ever, deviate from these principles of behavior. If and when they do, they take full responsibility through openness and self-awareness, and they make it right. By doing this, they generate the same kind of behavior from their employees, business partners, and customers. The old saying, "Do as I say and not as I do," never worked in parenting, and it sure doesn't work in leadership. Lead by example.

My *aikido* sensei is a model of this principle. He lives by a very clear set of values and fully demonstrates these values in our dojo (martial arts school). It creates a culture in our training and in the dojo where we, as students, learn to cultivate similar values over time. Those values then transfer into our lives outside the dojo. It is successful because my teacher "walks his talk." He's not playing at a value system. He lives his value system. It's a good thing his values are of the highest integrity. If they weren't, his students would not develop well. Does that mean that I agree with all of his opinions or actions? Of course not. It would be unrealistic to assume two thoughtful adults were perfectly aligned in all their beliefs. This is one of the reasons that many people don't accept the role of student as an adult. They can't deal with the human aspects of their teachers. The same is true for all areas of your life: your family, friends, and, of course, your business. It may also be that adults don't take on the role of student because too many stop being learners after they leave school. But if you've read this far in the book and you really want to go beyond booked solid, then you already know that you need to cultivate the "learner" part of your personality. If you do, you may begin to develop a "learning organization": a business that is in a constant state of growth through learning.

I keep referencing my teachers, the different people from whom I learn. I don't think many people have teachers as adults. We look at learning as an adolescent or young adult experience, not as something to do every day as an adult. I think most adults are more committed to doing things their way than they are to achieving their goals. I battle with this, too. So I just keep asking myself whether I'm more committed to my goal or my beliefs, behaving the way I've been behaving, doing things the way I've been doing them. Asking questions is the fundamental BS detector. Ask them of yourself—a lot. So what about you? Are you a learner? I hope so, because the future belongs to the learner, not the learned.

Which are you more committed to—your goals or your way of doing things?

Although our personalities don't change much, we can learn new ways of being, adopt new value systems and habits. Often it's really just rediscovering, cultivating, and nurturing traits you already possess. With these things in mind, you might want to go back to the sections on creativity and curiosity. I'm suggesting these things as ways to open up yourself, and possibly the people you hire, to new things. But don't hire people thinking that you can open them up with a few creativity exercises and end up molding them to a different or better personality type.

So, the leadership traits and values we want to develop are initiative and being in touch with your self and others (i.e., honesty, integrity, openness, self-respect, and treating people with dignity). The most effective way I know of to hone these traits and values is by taking on the responsibility of leadership. You can't cultivate leadership skills without actually serving others as a leader. That's the learning-in-action part. But don't forget that one of the key components of learning in action is the plus delta review and reflection. It's good to have a place where you go to see your reflection—a place where you can face yourself, not your idea of yourself, but how you actually are in the world. How your business is performing will be one important mirror of how you're doing as a leader. Am I retaining people? Is the business growing? Are the people who work with me growing? Each of these and more will be a reflection of how you are actually doing as a leader.

Your business, though, is only one part of the reflection. There needs to be an outside source as well, a place where you can see yourself for who you are. For me that's *aikido*. For you, it might be something else: a mastermind group, meditation, yoga, rock climbing, a business coach, or a thousand other things that offer a time for personal reflection. Here comes one of our mantras of the book again: working *on* your business, while working *in* your business and *on yourself*—this is the working *on yourself* part.

Ultimately leadership is about relationships. Actually, almost anything we want to accomplish in life is directly related, or proportionate, to our ability to develop and sustain healthy, mutually beneficial relationships. Of course, our first relationships are with our parents. Those relationships don't just color but also directly affect the way we relate to other people today. Even though I take more of an ontological (the study of being or the conceptions of reality), rather than a psychological, approach to coaching, both my parents are mental health professionals. My father is a psychiatrist, and my mother is a clinical social worker specializing in Early Childhood Development. No, it doesn't mean that I'm nuts. Nor does it mean that I'm perfect. I have learned many things from them, not the least of which has been to understand that my relationships early in life have often influenced the way that I behave in relationships today.

Until we see and understand how we're behaving in relationships and then let go of the negative aspects, it's difficult to truly be a great leader. Yes, many people have built impressive companies (big and profitable) while being totally dysfunctional. Do you want to be one of those people? I didn't think so. Incidentally, they may have built big companies, but more often than not they haven't achieved the all-important, as far as this book is concerned, work-life balance. If you can get over your relationship hang-ups and dysfunctionalities, you'll be able to relate to other people in a new and productive way. How much more confident you'll be once this happens. You'll be able to see others for who they really are (instead of through the lens of your own hang-ups)—and (as or more important) see yourself for who you truly are. We have one life. Work is part of it . . . a big part. So are our family, friends, hobbies, spirituality, and so on. It's the same for everyone. When you can relate to other people in terms of their essential nature, then people are freed up to take personal responsibility and to do remarkable things.

12 | Integrate— People and Process

There was a definite process by which one made people into friends, and it involved talking to them and listening to them for hours at a time.

—Rebecca West

How many times have you heard, or said, the phrase, "I just can't find good people." How long are you going to continue to look at the current and future health of your business as being based on finding people who fit an idea of what you need? Instead, consider this fact—great people need great systems to do great work, and great systems need great people to work well. But like anything, the challenge is determining how much "greatness" you need and can afford on each side of the scale. In this chapter, we look at how to strike that delicate balance between people and processes so the integration, or flow, between the two is seamless and effective.

People or Processes

It seems there are two schools of thought around this issue: There are those who think the solution is to hire the best people you can afford and continue to operate in chaos, without systems. Well, that's one way of avoiding the challenge of balancing and integrating— just don't bother. This is what might be called the people-centered approach to business building. It sounds very humanistic, but it isn't. Hiring people into chaos is like throwing a good swimmer into the middle of the ocean. Sure, he can swim. But to where? There's no land in sight for 100 miles or so and on the way there could be some little challenges like sharks, storms, not to mention exhaustion and dehydration. Systems are necessary, no matter how good people are.

Then there are those who say, create rigid process maps, document and systematize everything, and hire marginal people. Interesting. Not! It's just the flip side of the first coin and totally avoids finding the balance again. It's what is often called a systems-centered approach to business building.

This is a good place for me to take a short pause to introduce two systems concepts you may see referred to as you do further research into the issue: automation and autonomation. No, I didn't just misspell that second word or accidentally add extra syllables and no, they aren't the same thing. Not quite. Automation is the act of replacing human activities with a nonhuman device (machine, software program, etc.). Your calculator is an example. It automates the act of adding and subtracting and whatever other fancy math you might do. Excel spreadsheets can take it several steps further, performing complicated equations for you as you input data into different boxes. Autonomation, on the other hand, uses equipment that is endowed with human intelligence (think Hal ... and I mean *2001: A Space Odyssey,* not my friend Hal Macomber) to stop itself when it has a problem, so problems won't be passed on through the process. Autonomation works very well on an assembly line (car manufacturing and the like). It's unlikely that you will have any autonomic systems in your service business. The trick is to figure out how you can build the principle into your systems. It's all about the strength of your systems and finding the right balance with good people. A great system can alert a great person to a problem in the process.

There's no getting around it. You will need both great people and great systems, and you will have to balance those two. Remember satisficing? It may be that you start with good enough systems and good people, unless, of course, you have infinite resources, in which case, great, get the absolute best of both. The higher-level thinking suggests that you hire the best people and work with them to create the most effective processes for the business. But then you also need to create systems for finding the best people. Already the balancing is difficult. What's the cart and where's the horse, and until I know which is which, how do I know what goes first? You need to hold these two apparently contradictory thoughts in your head—people are the priority; systems are the priority—and work to move ahead simultaneously on both fronts. It's a constant balancing act.

Depending on your business architecture, the balance will be different. Franchising and network marketing, for example, require a lot of systems, and having the right processes is essential to the structure of the business—creating franchise agreements and franchise operating packages, developing the genealogy of sales commissions in a network marketing business. The "better mousetrap" and "train the trainer" might rely less on systems (though, of course, they still require them) and rely more on the people side of the equation.

I suggest you think about your balance between people and process something like the illustration in Figure 12.1. Each builds on the next and doesn't work without the other.

If you have a people- and process-related focus, rather just one or the other, you can create a culture for your business that changes work and work habits (see Figure 12.2).

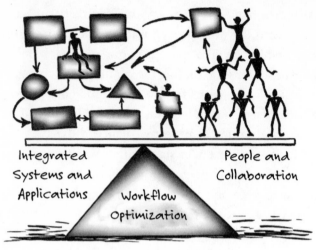

Figure 12.1   Scales

Integrated Systems and Applications

Workflow Optimization

People and Collaboration

Knowledge Management

Change Management

Skills Development

Collaboration

Governance

Incentive Systems

Lower Implementation Costs

Less Rework

Faster Benefits

Improved Benefits

More Aligned Workforce

Figure 12.2   Arrows

The Right Process Leads to the Right Results

People have misconceptions about their role in standardization:

Misconception #1: Managers or team leaders (you) often think standardization is about finding the one and only best way to do something and then freezing it.

Misconception #2: Team members often think that standardization is a coercive tactic designed to enforce rigid standards that will make their job boring and demeaning. They also assume that once what they do is standardized, they'll be replaced. If not immediately replaced, then they will be as soon as someone else is found who is cheaper.

In some cases, these may not be entirely misconceptions—at least for the team members. Freezing a standard no matter what or using a standard as a replacement for a good person may occur in some environments. But more often, the misconception is that a process is a negative thing to be fought against. Early on in my business, I had a team member who would not document her processes, no matter how many times I asked, begged, and pleaded. I spent hours coaching her on how to do it. I offered to hire someone to walk her through the process and essentially create the system for her . . . all to no avail. She eventually admitted to me that she thought that if she documented what she did, then I would just let her go. She seemed to think that standardizing might render her useless, as if it were somehow like mechanizing her job. Or maybe she thought that if I saw what she really did, I wouldn't think she was doing a good job. I told her that I wanted to standardize her tasks so her job would be easier and improve workflow throughout the organization. And furthermore, at this point, if she didn't document and standardize her tasks, I would be forced to hire someone to fill her shoes. Sadly, she didn't come around, and we parted ways. Of course, this was ultimately my responsibility for not testing an applicant's ability to document a process during the hiring process. I know better now and have built into the hiring process a system of testing the ability of potential new hires to document a number of tasks. That way I can assess in advance of hiring them if they can (and will) do it.

Your goal is to create enabling systems and procedures. You can think about this in the same way we thought about negative versus positive constraints earlier in the book. In fact, systems are constraints. They create ways of doing things that constrain people from doing things any old way. They also can create constraints that actually foster continuous improvement. While you may have some negative constraints left in your business that you could not eliminate, you should never have coercive systems. You create the systems, after all. It's in your control. With deference to P. S. Adler's article "Building Better Bureaucracies" in the *Academy of Management Executive* (November 1999), here's my simplified checklist of how to think about whether the systems you are creating are coercive or enabling:

- *Performance versus best practices:* A system that sets performance standards risks highlighting poor performance, without offering any constructive solution. Instead, create a system that focuses on best practices and how to achieve them. If you can provide people with the information and tools they need to do a good job, then the likelihood is that they will, if they can. Best practices guidelines are one of the surest ways to ensure good performance. If people know exactly what is expected of them, it's much easier for them to deliver what is expected. Without such guidelines a performance standard operates in a vacuum. Remember, each process must be designed to serve the conditions of satisfaction of that processes customer.
- *Standard versus custom:* It's true that you want to create a system that reduces the possibility of disorganized and irregular behavior and monitors costs to keep them low. But too much standardization can bind good people and prevent them from doing

the best job possible and eliminate the desire to continuously improve. It is better to build a system that allows some flexibility for good people to customize a process to suit their level of skill and experience. I don't mean a free-for-all, of course, just enough play in the system to enable people to work to their best potential.

- *Out of control versus in control:* Systems should not be used to control people. There is an idea that for processes to work effectively, employees need to be left out of the control loop. Not so. Systems should be there to help people control their work, not vice versa. When people have control of and understand the workflow they are part of, then they better understand the importance of their role and will perform better. This is what Adler calls a "glass box" system design. Just as it sounds, it means a system we can peek inside of, a process that is visible to everyone.

- *Ironclad instruction versus best practice:* That term again—best practices—it's an important concept. Systems in and of themselves should be templates for the best practices in your business. That's why they are always in a cycle of improvement. A best practice implies something that adapts to the future—new imperatives or new demands of the business. A system cannot be an ironclad rule to be followed and never challenged. It's not the army—although they tell me that even the army changes. You're creating dynamic systems in your growing, changing business.

Ideally, enabling systems foster extensive employee involvement, high levels of communication, innovation, flexibility, great morale, and a strong customer focus. Sounds like the perfect place to work.

Once again, though, the ideal enabling system contains two seemingly opposing principles. (1) You need to build information processes right the first time. It's much more effective and less costly than inspecting and repairing process and quality problems after the fact. (2) But once you've standardized and, thus, stabilized the process, the cycle of continuous improvement starts. Stability and change. Standard and flexible. Controlled and open. The challenge is to develop a learning organization that will constantly find ways to reduce waste and improve productivity.

A Place for Everything and Everything in Its Place

Here's another way to think about people, processes, and waste. *Waste is a constraint.* Reducing waste in your organization is one the easiest ways of reducing constraints. And here's a surprise—waste in offices is usually greater than in factories, especially because it's easy to hide waste in cumbersome or nonexistent processes. For example, when lots of inventory is kept in the office supply room (maybe that's your closet), you're naturally going to use more than you need and not pay attention to supplies running out. Creating unnecessary information inventory is another common waste in offices—doing too many tasks "in anticipation" of a possible client, for example.

In my business, I plan a lot of extended promotional campaigns. When I'm developing an eight-week campaign, I don't write out all the material in advance. Why? Because what happens in stages one and two can affect what I want to do in stage three. This is not to say that I don't plan in advance. On the contrary, what I do is scenario planning, that is, I imagine the different ways a campaign might go and make plans to develop certain scenarios, depending on which direction the actual campaign goes. Recently, I sent out a promotional e-mail for a seminar much farther in advance than I normally do. The response rate was significantly lower than I usually get for similar e-mails sent closer to the event date. So, I needed to adapt my next steps to reflect the low response rate. Had I written out all my promotional materials in advance, I would have wasted a lot of time developing a plan that I couldn't execute. Instead, I stayed flexible and kept my time freer to respond to reality.

One way to think about waste is in terms of push and pull systems. A *push system,* like much of traditional manufacturing, produces as much product as the company can and/or wants to produce and then gets it out to the customer. The result is usually large inventories. A *pull system* only produces what a customer needs and has asked for. Dell tried to do this with its "We'll custom build the computer for you." Ultimately, having a 100 percent pull system couldn't work for Dell. Unless you are a one-off couture designer to the stars, it's unlikely that a 100 percent pull system can work. But you want to have as much pull in your systems as you can. Toyota has very little excess inventory. That's why when the Prius was so unexpectedly popular, people found themselves on waiting lists for the car. Seems like a problem, but Toyota is much more profitable as a result of being so lean. You might also hear this concept referred to as just-in-time production, or JIT (remember?—it came from the supermarkets). I think of it this way—there's a place for everything and everything in its place. No more. No less.

SendOutCards.com uses a pull system for the most part. Aside from the digital designs, the printers, and a limited supply of card stock, envelopes, and stamps, the company doesn't hold excess inventory. Cards are printed as needed, as people generate a request to send them out from their desktops all around the world. The company can stay lean because it never produces product in advance of when it's ordered.

Push and pull systems are great examples of how to integrate people and process. When I was working in the fitness business, in charge of group exercise for a health club chain across the country, I instituted a pull system for staffing assistants in fitness classes. The way it worked before I got there was like this: For certain classes, both a teacher and an assistant were scheduled. Often sign-up for a class was below the threshold at which an assistant was needed, so the assistant who'd shown up was sent home, a waste of the assistant's time and a waste of the company's money. I implemented a process by which these classes had an "on-call" assistant. Based on the sign-up level an hour and a half before the class, a front desk staff member could determine whether the extra staff was required and call in an assistant. This gave the assistants time to come in, if needed, yet gave them the freedom to pursue their own activities in the event they weren't needed. And the clubs saved money because on-call assistants were only paid when needed. Incidentally, when I first introduced my idea for the system, people told me it couldn't be done. I asked, "Why?" Answer: Because it wasn't the way things had been done. So I kept asking "Why?" until the powers-that-be could not come up with another good reason not to try my idea. It was a case of "If you don't know anything, it's sometimes better because you aren't constrained by paradigm or policy." My new pull system worked well. Simple but effective.

Here's another story on how to reduce waste (figuratively and literally) by integrating people and process in a pull system. My *aikido* dojo is on the second (top) floor of a barn on a lavender farm with a view of a lake. It's as extraordinary as it sounds. We don't have a conventional toilet. Instead, there is an incinerator toilet. You first press a button to start the heating system and then put a special-purpose coated-paper bowl liner (like a coffee filter, but don't try using one for this purpose because it won't work) down between two sloping pieces of steel (sort of like a toilet bowl liner). You do "your business" into the paper filter, step onto a lever, and wave goodbye to your waste and any toilet paper. The toilet incinerates the filter and extra donations from you at a very high temperature, somewhere around 7,000 degrees Fahrenheit or the surface temperature of the sun, whichever is hotter. It's a great way to eliminate waste. However, you can't use the toilet without these special-purpose coated-paper bowl liners—they're needed to keep the steel clean while also aiding in the incineration process. Many have tried and have gotten a good scolding for it.

My teacher and his wife have implemented a very simple "pull system" so that we always have just the right number of liners—not too many, which ties up money and takes up extra space with excess inventory; and not too few, which can shut down the incinerator if it's overburdened by nonregulation uses. Not good. Over time my teacher and his wife have determined just how many boxes of this paper to keep on hand, based on the frequency of use. It happens to be four boxes. These boxes are then stacked on a specific shelf (the one closest to the toilet, not down the hall, which would create a different kind of production problem, but right where you need them—and can reach them). On the bottom box is written: *When you open this box, tell George or Patti.* You do tell them because it's built into the culture of the dojo and you are part of the smooth functioning of the system. They then order four more boxes and have determined, through learning by doing, just how long it takes to receive a shipment. It's a very simple pull system that, in this case, only produces the right kind of waste.

As you can tell, there are a number of keys to success in this process. Everything about this process is clearly *visible* (apparent) to everybody involved in the process. If the box marked *When you open this box, tell George or Patti* was inside a dark, hard-to-reach cabinet, or if the statement was written on the bottom of the box instead of on the flap that you have to open to get at the liners, it might not get noticed. The process relies on this *visual indicator*. Visual indicators, management charts, or checklists allow for communication and sharing. You can create standardized work sheets but if you don't have a way of seeing them, and the process, as if it were in a glass box, it's likely that the standard practice won't be followed and breakdown and waste will occur.

Take filing cabinets, for example. If you file your papers in an enclosed filing cabinet in the basement, it's unlikely you know what's in it and whether you are putting the right things in it. I'm not naturally good at filing and other organizational kinds of work, so I've had to create new habits that force me to be more productive, like keeping a three-foot-long open-top filing cabinet adjacent to my desk so I can see into it. Same things for my books, bills, and other paperwork, as well as the way files and documents are organized on my computer— I need to see them, to keep them top-of-mind, or I ignore them.

By the way, I'm not the only person in the world who needs things in sight to be on top of them. David Allen (of the Getting Things Done system) advocates strongly for an open filing system for things you are using on a regular basis. Again, these are called *visual indicators*. Of course, it's easier to ignore things that are disagreeable, but that's not helpful to doing big things in the world.

Problems have a way of bubbling up to the surface. The longer you let them simmer, the bigger the problem will be when it surfaces. Our goal is to create standardized work processes that bring issues and problems to the surface (using visual indicators so no problems are hidden) at the earliest possible moment. People are stimulated by the visual, tactile, and audible. People are part of the process. Remember, we're integrating. So it stands to reason that being able to see everything you manage is a balanced and harmonious way of creating flow in your work.

Don't Overwork People

I've been guilty of overworking people. One of the benefits of creating standardized workflows related to customer or client demand is that you can level the workload. If you reduce waste, unevenness, excess burden on one person, you create a lean operation where people can continuously improve—themselves and the organization.

The service business seems to come inherently with a lot of waste, unevenness, and overburdened people. It's one of the reasons you may get overwhelmed and frustrated with the work you're doing, particularly once you're booked solid. We've talked a lot about how to reduce waste. Let's look now at how to level out workloads so you don't overwork yourself and others—one of the most significant causes of burnout and poor production.

The key is to fit customer demand into a leveled schedule (remember, there are two types of customers: internal and external). At certain times of the day, or week, or month, do certain activities—the way dentists do. Have you ever noticed how organized dentists are? They always seem to know how long things are going to take, and they schedule accordingly. Mondays might be root canal day and Tuesday wisdom teeth day. That's because dentists establish different time allotments for different types of procedures. Contractors do (or I should say "should" do, since I see little evidence of organizational ability among the contractors I seem to use) the same. Establish standard times for delivering different types of services. Yes, sometimes it is the clients who bring in new and hidden variables that muck up the standard timing, but over time even the unexpected can be accounted for. If you have standard workflow charts and your systems are visible, then you should have a very good idea of how long things take, too. From there it's simply a matter of calculating the resources you have (including you) and how much you can deliver, when. This goes back to our earlier discussion of turnaround times. Not everything needs to be responded to in 24 hours. It is better to establish standard, longer, response periods and occasionally surprise a client with faster service. When you set an expectation of, say, a 48-hour response time, when you respond more quickly, people will be pleasantly surprised instead of unimpressed because, let's face it, everyone nowadays seems to think things should happen instantly.

If you don't know how long things take, then you need to back up and work on your systems some more.

People versus Technology

Systems can reduce waste, of course. That's what this whole module is about. But they can also, as you've seen, be sources of waste. Unless you have a problem-solving process in place and people who are following it, there's very little value in spending time or money on fancy technology.

Customer relationship management (CRM) software is a classic example of this kind of "If we buy it, we'll figure out how to use it" technology. A few years ago, it seemed like that acronym was everywhere. Bottom line, there's a lot of dusty CRM software. I've got some myself. You can't expect people to suddenly become customer service or sales process oriented just because they have the software. CRM is, in the end, a human process; it won't work unless you have humans who already understand this and are already engaged in a customer support process. CRM software, like all technology, can improve or help, not create.

Technology is not a system in and of itself. It requires people to put it in motion, to use it to its greatest effect. Yet often we get sucked into wanting the latest and greatest, whatever it is and whether we have a use for it. I'm so guilty of this. I love technology and often fantasize that all process problems can be solved with it. Some can, sure; but if you adopt new technology before you have a culture that reduces waste, problem solves, thinks lean, and has standardized all its operations, you might just create more issues to contend with. If that's the case, frankly, there's really no point in adding new technology. This is by no means an excuse not to add new technology when necessary. It's merely a caution. Use the best tools your money can buy, but make sure you know exactly what you're going to improve and how you're going to improve it with new technology. And make sure you can measure your success with the new technology.

If you've made it this far in the book, chances are that you are already internalizing the idea that you need to be constantly innovating, implementing, measuring, and improving, with the object of integrating the people and processes in your business in the best way possible. Why? So you can build a bigger, better business, of course. But that's only one of the reasons. The other equally important reason is that by effectively integrating people and processes, you will free yourself up for . . . well, read on.

13 | Live—
The Balance

There is more to life than increasing its speed.
—Mohandas K. Gandhi

What's it all for, all this right attitude, business architecture, and systems? What is your destiny, inside and outside of your business? If you serve others, but don't serve your own destiny, things are going to fall apart. Often people get trapped into doing a job, providing a service that they've been praised for but that they don't enjoy. They continue to "serve" because they think it's the "right" thing to do. But they are just using their skills, without being true to their purpose.

It isn't easy having both a successful business and a rich personal life, but it is possible if you are aligned with your larger goals and your vision for your life. You *can* have your business and your life in your way. There will be times when you push hard at work, but there need to be times when you put energy into other areas of your life. Ultimately, the goal is to not push too hard on one (usually the business) and completely neglect the other. Implement a system for your life, call it a "life model," to use as a guideline that will enable you to achieve your destiny. Your dream was never to work every waking minute with no time for family, friends, hobbies, health-promoting activities, or holidays, was it? Creating systems for your business will ultimately free up more of your time. Learn how to use your free time wisely.

A couple I know from my acting days are an interesting example of the lengths to which we can go to find balance. She was an actor and a writer. He was a hugely successful financial type. First they lived in London, where he worked obsessively. Then he was offered the chance to run a hedge fund in Bermuda (with a financial package they thought he couldn't refuse), and they moved there so he could continue to work obsessively. He wasn't happy, just obsessed. Finally, she said she wanted to move back to the United States with the children. Amazingly, he quit his job to go with her because he realized that his life balance had gotten too far out of whack and that he was going to lose his marriage and family. He wasn't serving his destiny and things were falling apart. Long story short, he followed his dream to become a farmer, investing what he'd made working in the financial business into an organic cattle farm. And I don't mean that he became a gentleman farmer who sips martinis and surveys his land from afar. He became the kind of farmer who gets up at 5 A.M. and spends his time with the animals. He saved his marriage and his relationship with his children. Now he and his wife work together. Because of his ability to change and to recognize that things were out of balance, he is doing something he loves and so is his wife. In other words, he's now happy as a pig in . . .

Finding Flow

Most of us will find the life balance right for us by taking somewhat less extreme measures. I think about this balance in three ways. I don't want to call them "steps." Though they follow one from the other, they are more integrated with each other than that. They are:

1. *Be in line with your purpose.* What do you want to do with your life? Who do you want to be?
2. *Pay attention to the harmony in the world around you.* Are you and your actions harmonious with your purpose, with others, and with the broader world?
3. *Find flow in your business and in your life.* The more flow there is in how you work and how you live, the more time you will spend in what's called "the zone"—that place where hard things become easy, rough things smooth.

The idea of flow was first introduced in Mihaly Csikszentmihalyi's book *Flow: The Psychology of Optimal Experience.* Since then many others have built on the idea of flow and the zone. Athletic coaches in particular have picked up on the concept, and it's not uncommon to hear an athlete describe an experience of being in flow, of being in the zone during a particularly important and challenging event. But flow is not just about sports; it's about your whole life, professional and personal. In business, flow is about creating a level, or even, work flow so that our business grows smoothly and we have time for the other parts of our life. It's what this whole book has been about so far. Learning how to remove and apply constraints, to create systems, and to do projects with other people are the tools by which you can establish the level work flow.

Balanced, level flow will make you better at what you do (in other words, it's good for business!). It is the pursuit of mastery that we've talked about before. A master in *aikido* doesn't get tired, no matter how grueling the sequence the master does. Why? Because the *aikido* master is always in flow. It's what makes a master. Level flow is about eliminating the need for all-nighters. It is finding the way to work and to live that doesn't exhaust us and others. Your level workflow will not only help your business because you are working more efficiently and effectively, but it allows you to develop other people without burning them out. It allows you to treat customers better and to deliver your services better because you are not burned out. You've probably seen how it can happen—an entire organization can shift into adrenaline mode because a few key people are working that way instead of working in flow. We've heard the stories about surgeons operating on the wrong limb and about how people going in for knee surgery will take a big magic marker and write "not this knee" on one knee and "this knee" on the other. We don't want this in our business or in our lives—and certainly not in the operating room. It's not balanced.

There are many different opinions on balance. At the turn of the century (the early 2000s, but it was more fun to say it that way), there seemed to be a book a week about balance. The problem was—balance often meant that a person was spending too much time on their weaknesses. Marcus Buckingham's *Now, Discover Your Strengths,* refined balance and helped us understand that we should spend more time on our strengths. It just makes sense. Tim Ferriss's idea of the four-hour workweek is another great take on balance and reminds us that working harder than anyone else is not the right balance, nor is it a life. It's sometimes hard not to work too hard. I know. I have to work hard to keep myself from working too hard. I'm a maximizer. I'm ambitious. My problem isn't that I dabble in things, and it's probably not your issue either if you've read this far in the book. You're probably like me, prone to obsess. Don't. Please don't let all the great new strategies and techniques you've learned in this book become your new obsession. Then I won't have helped you. Balance, harmony, level work flow, however you want to think about it, comes down to mastery. Masters don't get tired. Their energy flow nourishes itself. They understand flow and balance.

No surprise—balance is different for every one of us. We are each unique (I know that's not news). We each have different things that turn us on. For me, it's speaking. I can do a one-hour talk and it feels like one minute because it's so much fun. So I design my business to include speaking. But I can't do it every day. There are other things

I need to weigh into the balance—the wear and tear of the travel to get to speaking engagements, my family, the other parts of my business that need my attention, my goal to be in my dojo 10 hours a week with my sensei (not just in any old dojo that I can find in my travels). To achieve the life balance that's right for me, that keeps me in a level flow, I speak only a few times per month, and then I create other ways to deliver my services without traveling. What the right life model is for you depends not only on what jazzes you but also on your stage of life.

Balance is not about taking time to smell the flowers, though if that's what you love then it may be part of the balance for you. Taking a month off from your business might be a great goal, or it might not. It's ultimately about having control over your future. Level flow does not mean that you operate at the same energy level all the time. The opposite in fact—it's about creating natural cycles of effort and rest (that's where having control of your future is important). There may be times when you exhaust yourself, but those need to be planned and followed by periods where you take time off. Before I started bike racing, I used to go out and ride hard every time I got on my bike. The result was that I wasn't improving and I was constantly exhausted. Once I started racing, I had something to work toward. I became disciplined about being in harmony with the universe, finding the natural flow of my energy peaks and valleys. Before I give a speech, I need to be careful not to try to create a particular energy. Instead I tap into the audience's energy. We all need to tap into the energy of the people we're working with. There's only so long you can be an energetic cheerleader for a project if the people around you need to be manipulated into corresponding energetic responses. I'm sure you've all felt how your energy level rises around people who are excited about the work they are doing or, for that matter, how your energy lifts with someone who has a zest for life.

High energy is great, but more important is the level flow. We need to understand that our energy levels, not just physical, but mental, too, have ebbs and flows. Here's a cool fact: Our bodies operate on a biological cycle called the Body-Rest-Activity-Cycle (BRAC). The length of the cycle varies between 90 and 120 minutes. Basically, you can perform at your peak for no more than one of these cycles before you start to push your limits. If you try too often to extend your high activity levels, you'll experience exhaustion in the short term, and over the longer term, you'll burn out. Athletes, like my bike racing friends, understand this better than many people. Business owners often ignore it because they don't experience physical manifestations, and they don't realize the mental and emotional toll of working too long and too hard, without respite. By the time the physical breakdown happens, it's way too late.

Have a Hobby

So how do we begin to establish balance? My mother, Vivian Port (as I mentioned), is a clinical social worker. Her specialty is Early Childhood Development. One of the things she does is encourage parents to support their children in developing hobbies. Note that I said "support" not push or force their children into activities in hopes that they'll develop into hobbies. That's a no-no. Her belief (and from what I understand, the research supports this) is that children who have hobbies become adults who have hobbies and that people with hobbies tend to be happier and more successful people. It's not too late for you to get yourself a hobby or to rekindle a hobby. But again, it needs to be something you want to do naturally. You can't force yourself on a hobby. Think of pastimes you enjoy and wish you could spend more time doing. Support yourself in finding more time to do them. Oh, but how do I find more time? You have it already and if you've been working through this book, you have probably already found at least a few more hours in every week, if not in every day. Not only can you save $18,000 a year, but you'll have more time for hobbies.

I used to have the opposite problem. I was an actor. (My first career. You can see some of my credits if you search on my name at imdb.com. I had only a modicum of success.) But I never knew when I was going to be working and when I'd have free time. Maybe my agent would call and I'd have an audition that afternoon, or maybe the audition would be in four days. I had a lot of free time, but I never knew when I was going to get it. I could have become a person who just watched a lot of TV. But that's not leveling the flow; that's shutting it off. There's a difference between rest and opting out of your life. Sure, a little television isn't going to kill you, but the cycles of level flow aren't activity and passivity, they're peaks and valleys of energy and activity. Enough said. I developed hobbies, bike racing and *aikido,* that I was able to pursue whenever I had free time, without having to schedule them in advance. My hobbies were as flexible as I needed to be. And what my hobbies did for me was to even the flow in my life. Instead of having down days where I cooled my heels waiting for something to happen, I profited on the slow days by getting in some cycling and some *aikido* practice. For me, the problem was that ultimately I preferred my hobbies to my job. I kept hoping not to get auditions so I could cycle instead. That's when I realized that I needed to find a new line of work. Balance is enjoying work and everything else, not dreading one or the other.

Having hobbies, interests outside of work, helps even the flow of both by creating outlets for your energy on down days and by creating incentives to work more efficiently. Hobbies are not a waste of time or a way of killing time until the next "real" responsibility comes along. Hobbies are a key way we achieve balance. As soon as we recognize the importance of balance, we can redefine what it means to be productive and to contribute meaningfully.

I have a friend whose father works as a labor arbitrator. He has the same challenges I had as an actor. Labor arbitrations are scheduled months in advance, but during those months, the parties try to settle their differences without having to resort to arbitration. That means that as late as the night before, an arbitration day can be cancelled. The fee still gets paid, but my friend's father suddenly has a free day to fill. He can, of course, spend some of that time trying to drum up new business or working *on* his business in some other way, but he's also lucky enough to have hobbies, which even the flow, too. He's an amateur photographer and he plays the clarinet. His hobbies are ready for him whenever he's ready for them. It wasn't always that way for him. In the beginning, he found it stressful to take days off at a moment's notice. He would be frustrated by not feeling productive. But then he discovered and rediscovered things he'd always wanted to do, and now he relishes his unexpected days off as much as his days of work. He has a balance and flow that work for him.

Having an incentive to work more efficiently can work magic. Think about the typical week before you go on vacation. You put your nose to the grindstone and work energetically to get things done. You clear out your e-mail inbox and return phone calls you'd been avoiding. You pay bills, send out invoices, and resolve nagging customer service issues. You distribute enough work to your employees to keep them busy while you are gone. You don't waste time chatting or surfing the Internet. In other words, you are superproductive, a model of efficiency. Check. Check. Check. Check. Your to-do list shrinks and disappears.

Who was that superproductive, whirlwind? It was you—before vacation. As productivity guru David Allen (the Getting Things Done guy) says, "Isn't it interesting that people feel best about themselves right before they go on vacation?" They've cleared up all of their to-do piles, closed up transactions, and renewed old promises with themselves. So you know you can do it.

Maybe that level of frenetic activity is just that—frenetic, as in, not sustainable. You can do it for only so long, and then you burn out. So, are you really enjoying your vacation as much as possible if you get there so exhausted it takes four days to wind down? Earlier, we talked about leveling the workload, establishing systems that ensured no one individual was overburdened. That means you, too. How can you maintain that prevacation productivity without burning out? Balance, harmony, level the flow. Your vacation is part of the larger cycle of your energy peaks and valleys. There's no getting around the fact that you will experience higher work energy right before a vacation. It's inevitable. The objective is to create that kind of cyclical balance the rest of the time, too.

My first and most basic suggestion: Be that prevacation person more than once a year. I don't just mean take more than one vacation, though that's a good goal, too. I mean behave that way, even if you aren't going to Europe, or Disneyland, or the Caribbean next week. *Schedule fun once a day—after your normal working schedule.* Fun, as in something you like to do outside of work, as in a hobby, an outside interest . . . what we talked about before. Fun is part of the level flow of your life. Fun is also an important source of creativity. Remember, creativity is at the root of all the changes you're going to make in your business. You need to have the mental space and energy for creativity. Having balance and level flow (and therefore some fun time) will help your creative juices flow, too.

Scheduling fun is a way of creating a constraint. It is another way of forcing yourself to squeeze waste out of the way you are working. We all have a lot of waste in the way we produce work product. For years, I've been hosting a free Think Big Revolution conference call every Monday at noon Eastern time. (Learn more at ThinkBigRevolution.com.) Each week I introduce a topic that I think will help the callers think big about who they are and what they offer the world. I used to routinely take an hour and a half to prepare my notes for the conference call and to write the e-mail notice I sent out. I realized that I was spending far more time than I ought to preparing for the conference call. I made a rule for myself. I was only allowed 15 minutes to make my notes and write the e-mail. The amazing thing is that my notes and e-mail are as good as they've always been. It turned out that I was filling the time because I thought I ought to or because the time was there. When I placed a time constraint on myself, I was able to produce the same work in less time.

It won't always be possible, but you'll be surprised by how often a simple thing like a time constraint can focus your mind on a project. It's just another form of deadline. That one small constraint gifted an hour and a quarter to my life each week, more time to get other things done, to devote to *aikido*, or to spend with my son.

Exercise

What things do you love to do (besides working and spending time with your family)? Are there things you used to do? Why aren't you doing them now? "Oh, I couldn't do them now," is not an answer. There are very few things that you used to do that you can't do now, if you really think about it. "I was younger then," you might think. So what? There are adult classes and clubs for just about any activity you can think of, no matter how "childish" you imagine it to be (and the whole concept of categorizing certain things as childish activities is questionable anyway). Make a list of the things you love to do, things you used to do, things you wish you could do. Pick the one that calls out to you the most. Research how you could take it up again. That might mean finding a club, finding a teacher, finding a location, or finding a piece of equipment. Figure out how you could participate in that activity again.

Learning to create a way of being in the world that is in harmony with the universe and in continuous flow is the most important thing you can do for yourself. Each of the things we've looked at for building a bigger, better business is applicable to our life balance, too. That's why I suggested that you read through the whole book once first, before you plunged into making changes. As you remove and apply constraints in your business, think about how they will affect the rest of your life. As you create systems, consider their wider impact, and consider how you might develop similar systems outside work. As you work with others to complete projects, think about the projects you want to complete in the rest of your life, and apply the same tools to those projects. The more even our work flow, the more level we are emotionally, the easier it is to be reflective, to think long-term about our business and our life, so that we can serve others in our businesses and serve our destiny. You *can* control your future. What do you want?

14

Case Studies—
Real People,
Real Businesses

Theory without experience is sterile, practice without theory is blind.

— *George Jay Anyon*

Chances are if you've made it this far, you've already started to think about, if not act on, the ideas in this book. You're on your way to moving beyond booked solid. But there's one last piece of the puzzle I think you'll find helpful. How exactly have others done it? You've seen bits and pieces, hints of how it's been accomplished in other businesses, but you probably want to see it all in one place. How did any one particular person move beyond booked solid? I'll do one better for you. In this chapter, we look at case studies of service professionals in all sorts of different businesses who have gone beyond booked solid. It's nothing academic or scientific, rather they are stories of what other people have done that can serve as a reference or a starting point for you, so that you can see a way into what is possible.

179

Their names will be familiar to you by now, as will some of their stories. Here you'll have a chance to see how each of them innovated, designed a new architecture, and put the systems in place to sustain the business into the future. And you'll see how they, some better than others, managed the work-life balance.

Very few of these entrepreneurs took a perfectly straight course to building their new business architecture. Nor was the journey always easy and free of roadblocks and potholes. They got messy and skinned a few knees along with way. I wouldn't expect it to be any other way. They faced, and will continue to face, significant challenges, including times of great stress, anxiety, and doubt. Some of them have built enormous businesses from nothing, but they don't have the work-life balance down yet. Some have built more slowly, but they've already achieved the work-life split they want. What sets these people apart is that they have all persevered. It is more important to them to do something great than to do something ordinary. Which would you prefer? They built their businesses without knowing all the answers before they began. They came from disparate backgrounds, many with no entrepreneurial experience or education. Yet, taken together, I found that these eight strategies and principles recurred as consistent contributors to success across the case studies:

1. *Openness:* They were open to challenges and said, "Yes!" to opportunities. When preparation meets opportunity much is possible.
2. *Urgency:* They had a powerful and urgent drive and desire to move forward now.
3. *Risk taking:* They wanted to go big or go home. They put their actions behind their words.
4. *Mentorship:* They avoided obstacles and overcame hurdles by soliciting advice from experts.
5. *Flexibility:* They adjusted to change in their marketplace and in the needs of their customers.

6. *Collaboration:* They were willing to collaborate with others (but not abdicate or delegate) to share responsibilities.
7. *Systems:* They were able to replicate procedures and to create processes for others to execute.
8. *Metrics:* They tracked effort versus results and adjusted accordingly.

Now let's meet some canny entrepreneurs and get to some inspiring stories.

Brandon Hartsell and Sunstone Yoga

Brandon Hartsell didn't start out his professional life expecting or even imagining that he would be a yoga teacher, let alone an entrepreneur in the health and wellness industry. Now he owns Sunstone Yoga, which is comprised of not one, but a string of popular yoga studios in Dallas, Texas. Founded in 2002, his studios have consistently been named as Best in Dallas.

Brandon started his career playing basketball professionally in Croatia and Germany. He went on to get a degree in economics and an MBA, along the way working as a financial analyst for various start-up companies. Yoga was always part of his life, so eventually he took the next step and became a yoga teacher, giving classes at a variety of studios. As he got deeper into teaching, he developed a better understanding of the yoga industry and what he thought was missing.

So he opened his own studio to offer yoga the way he thought it should be taught. He made sacrifices and took big risks. He and his business partner, Nicole Shaw, put virtually every penny they had into the budding business. They lived in the studio for the first year to save money on rent, and they each taught 15 to 18 classes per week (maybe the yoga helped them maintain a peaceful outlook with so much at stake). They started small; yet from the beginning, they had a clear vision of the future growth opportunities and put systems in place to ensure a smooth operation that provided both excellent customer service and a great place to work. The systems facilitated expansion. They made business decisions based on scalability and excellence—the ability to offer the same thing with the same quality to many more people (Figure 14.1).

Remember when we talked about the four criteria for going beyond booked solid: profitability, scalability, excellence, and leverage? Brandon figured it all out along the way. You'll be three steps ahead when you start after you've read this book. As Brandon says, "When you're building a business, you want to look at whether something is going to be scalable; it's just second nature to me to take into account those considerations. By building one studio with those considerations, you're building a system that can support an unlimited number of studios." Thinking ahead meant he and Nicole didn't chase after every good idea, but rather stuck close to their original vision.

Leverage, too, was important. So Brandon and Nicole built the business in such a way that it wouldn't rely on either of them to be the primary service providers. Once the first studio was getting booked solid, they created a teacher-training program to develop new teachers for the studio. With that one idea, they achieved four things: (1) created an additional source of revenue, (2) ensured the consistent high quality of teachers at the studio, (3) provided teachers with a place to work, and (4) built the foundation for a future franchise business, operated by their trained teachers who could in turn teach the Sunstone method.

One of the drawbacks of most yoga teacher-training courses, according to Brandon, is that they aren't able to help teachers actually find jobs once they're certified. As he says, "When you're offering a teacher-training program, you have to create the places for them to teach. That means that it's not enough just to teach them a skill set. If you don't provide the opportunity when you send somebody out

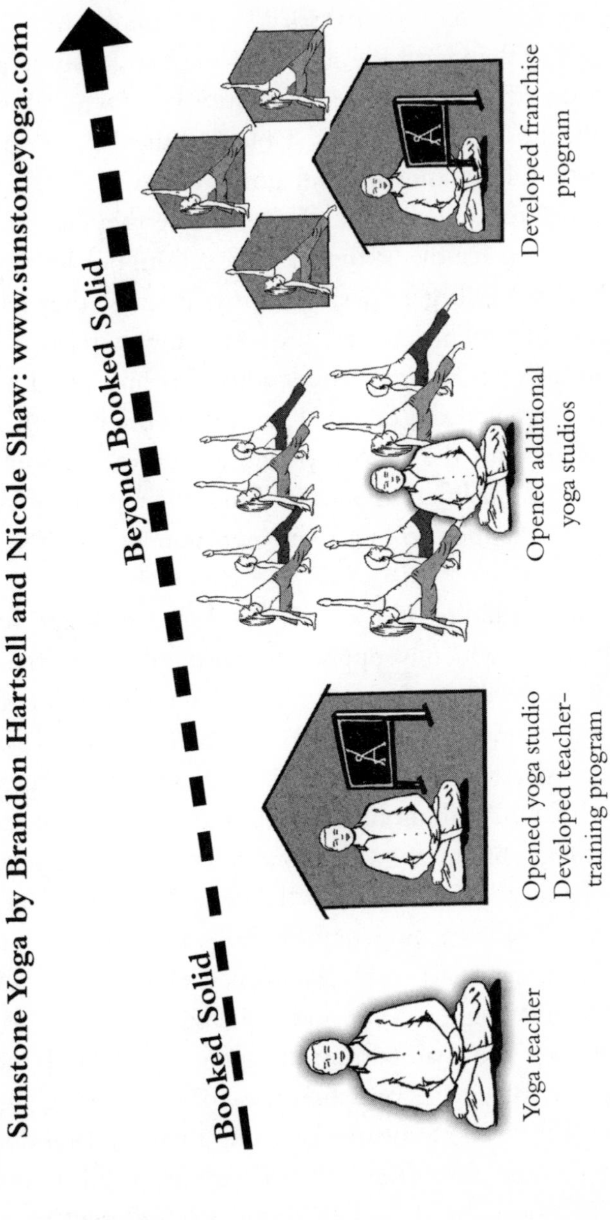

Figure 14.1 Yoga

from your school, their chance of survival is very low. In fact, they probably won't succeed. Most don't, and the life cycle of their attempt will probably be about six months. So, if you're not creating facilities [for them to teach] then it's not going to work [for the students/new teachers]. You could say, well, there's facilities out there where they can teach, but if those facilities aren't stable, and they're not offering a good product, then how long are they going to last?"

Sunstone Yoga expanded quickly, not because they had more clients than they could handle at their first location, but because they wanted to. They had an urgent desire to grow. Because they had been vigorous about documenting their processes and systems from day one, they were able to replicate the studios fast and build a bigger enterprise. They opened the first few studios themselves. Once they were comfortable with the success of the expansion, they offered a program to which qualified applicants from their pool of certified Sunstone teachers applied to buy their own franchise of a Sunstone Yoga Studio.

This franchise building block is the big-picture design for their business architecture, which is supported by using the train-the-trainer building block to develop a base of potential franchisees. Franchising provides an opportunity for Sunstone's certified teachers to become owners of their own studios without competing with Sunstone, instead partnering with them. With more studios, Brandon and Nicole can provide people throughout the city with easy access to the Sunstone teaching methods. The better the franchisees do, the better Sunstone does overall. It also provides more teaching opportunities for certified Sunstone teachers who don't want to own their own studios. And it builds the Sunstone brand, increasing revenue and reducing risk.

One of the keys to maintaining the integrity of the franchise is Brandon's system of checks and balances to ensure that all teachers are implementing the Sunstone teaching method. Brandon periodically drops in on classes, and all teachers are subject to regular peer review. Brandon also does something very different from other yoga studios: Every Sunstone studio posts class schedules, but it never posts who will be teaching. In this way, yoga students commit to the Sunstone class, not to a particular teacher, and all teachers need to meet the expectations of the Sunstone students. This technique also ensures that students are spread more evenly across the available classes (remember level flow?).

Part of the Sunstone business method (as opposed to the yoga method) is the commitment to metrics. Through disciplined tracking of their customers' purchasing habits, they can understand their clients' needs and desires and make better decisions. It helps, for example, with their expansion as they forecast future trends in the yoga market. To stay on top of the metrics, Sunstone exploits software programs for project management, increasing levels of accountability. Your ability to grow your business is in large part based on your ability to complete projects. Surprising as it is, many people don't know how to do projects with others. The Sunstone team gets things done. Brandon and Nicole train and rely on talented, decent people who are willing to implement and improve the Sunstone systems, methods, and philosophy.

Brandon describes the architecture they've built this way, "Our business model is based on an equilateral triangle—students on one side, teachers on another, and franchising on the third side. If any one of those sides grows disproportionately, then our triangle gets unequal and so the other sides have to catch up."

Ron Quintero and My Resource Center, Mortgage Leaders Edge, Debt Advisory Alliance, and Finance This Home

Ron Quintero is the founder of My Resource Center, Mortgage Leaders Edge, Debt Advisory Alliance, and Finance This Home—all businesses that serve professionals in the real estate industry. It wasn't always this way for Ron. He grew up in the foster care system, and he's spent time living on the streets. He never graduated from high school. But Ron is tenacious. He made it off the streets into a job with UPS. He had job security and benefits and was earning a decent wage. But it wasn't enough for him. Nor was it enough for the woman he wanted to marry.

There comes a point (sometimes more than one) in every relationship where it moves forward to the next level or it ends. Ron wanted his relationship to move forward. The good news for Ron was that his girlfriend wanted it to move forward, too, but only if he did. So one day she spelled it out for him: "I have bigger goals, dreams, and aspirations for you." Ron's girlfriend wanted him to reach for more, to not settle into one job for life. Ron realized he did, too. He was capable of more. He could think bigger about who he was and what he had to offer. He needed to move beyond just worrying about job security.

Ron took a big risk—he quit his job to pursue a career as a real estate agent. In the process, he blew his savings, and his home went into foreclosure—but he got the girl . . . and the business. Ron made it through the dip. He got booked solid as a real estate agent (Figure 14.2).

Then he met the man who would become his mentor. Ron says, "I had the good fortune to meet a man by the name of Tom Hopkins. He exposed me to the spiritual side of my life, and I kind of saw him as a father figure. He took me under his wing and started giving me advice when I was 21, 22 years old coming up through the real estate ranks. He took time to give me extra attention and point me in the right direction."

Ron began to purchase realty franchises, and from there went on to purchase a number of other related businesses—an escrow company, a mortgage company, a real estate licensing school, a property management company, a home owners' insurance company, and an appraisal firm. Once he had systematized these businesses, he sold almost all of them and moved on, creating a real estate firm that was a total solution provider. The business sold the homes and provided the financing and many other services—the whole nine yards.

Figure 14.2 Quintero

When the market in his region, Orange County, took a downturn, Ron adapted to the foreclosure market, differentiating himself by his flexibility and ability to prosper in the tough times. Ron became the "go to" person within this market. As he says, "I think that the *Book Yourself Solid* mindset is what we adopted early on. It's about becoming a specialist versus a general practitioner. In the real estate space, what we realized was, yes, we bought a franchise, but at the same time they were teaching the concept of being a general practitioner, trying to be everything to everybody, looking for an opportunity to say yes at every turn. What *Book Yourself Solid* does more than anything else, in my opinion, is teach people to think about, what is my niche, what is it that I do that makes me unique and separates me from the group? How can I not fall into the commodity trap? How can I not be a person who is being compared against others, for services that are seen, in the consumer's eye, as the same as everybody else's?" At this, Ron succeeded. Ron built up so much experience in the real estate market that people started to ask him to share his knowledge with them. He decided to sell off his remaining businesses so he could dedicate himself to training others.

What made this possible? All of his businesses were fully systematized, and those systems were documented so others could work the systems. Ron believes in basing his business decisions on metrics. He is a Six Sigma (a process to improve processes) black-belt certified trainer and describes his views on balancing people management with process management like this: "Combining the right people with the right process and then measuring what's going on within those environments is how I'm able to make decisions that will improve the development of the business. I have spreadsheets like you wouldn't believe!"

Ron knows that good systems are essential to the success of his business. His systems include accountability spreadsheets, project sheets, and goal sheets for each department. If breakdown occurs, he looks at the spreadsheet first, not the people. So his team members don't feel singled out or personally attacked.

With good systems in place that ensure the integrity of the business operation, Ron can focus on strategic alliances, a key part of his business strategy. He says he would have focused on alliances sooner if he had fully understood the power of the approach. Now, 40 percent of his marketing initiatives are based on joint ventures. He has 11 marketing partners. As he now says, "If you can find a way to be an asset to help drive business to your referral partners, than you too will receive referrals."

Like the others we'll meet in these case studies, Ron has a sense of urgency about his work and the growth of his business. He learns in action. He says, "I didn't have all the answers. I let those I work with know that I didn't know what it was going to look and feel like. But we are going to learn this together. If you want to go on this journey together, then let's do that. I think a lot of people appreciated that honesty. A lot of people said, Okay, that's just part of the journey, and they jumped on, and they said we are all learning together; let's make it happen. I was always determined."

Mike Berkley and the Berkley Center for Reproductive Wellness and Women's Health

Mike Berkley is an acupuncturist and the founder of the Berkley Center for Reproductive Wellness and Women's Health, a chain of wellness centers that specialize in treating men's and women's infertility using acupuncture, herbal medicine, yoga, meditation, nutrition, and other modalities. Like many of the people profiled in this book, he started his career in a very different place—as a computer salesman.

Of his time as a computer salesman, he says,

"My sole justification for waking up in the morning was to see how many computers I could sell at the end of the day. That's what the sole justification of many people's existence is in one

way or another. I am not at all religious, but one day I was
watching a program about some saint. This woman was standing
in the middle of the town taking her clothing off, piece by piece
and handing the clothes to people who needed clothing. Then
her friends tried to stop her and said, 'You can't do this, you're
going to be thrown in jail, you can't take your clothes off in
the middle of town. Are you crazy?' The woman responded by
saying, 'All that is not given is lost.' I realized that my life was
only about getting and not about giving, and a bunch of things
happened at that time. I had a very good friend who was an
acupuncturist, and I was talking to him about acupuncture—
I didn't think I had any interest in it at the time, but then a
couple of days later I was reading the *Village Voice*, which was a
paper that I never read before, and I saw an ad that read: Pacific
College of Oriental Medicine, a San Diego–based acupuncture
school is pleased to announce its opening. I decided to go to
this open house. I stayed for six years until I opened my own
practice. Acupuncture and herbal medicine is a business that
allows me to serve people greatly on a daily basis and allows me
to generate income for my family. So, I segued from computers
to acupuncture based on this lightning that hit me when this
saint said, 'All that is not given is lost.' I just ended up following
my bliss, and here I am." (See Figure 14.3.)

Much of Mike's success can be attributed to his decision to focus
on a niche market. As with most other practitioners, he started as a
generalist, treating everything from foot pain to headaches, chronic
coughs to insomnia. After being in practice for about a year and a half,
a chain of events motivated him to dedicate himself and his practice
to treating only fertility issues. That's what he's been doing since 1996.
Since becoming a specialist, he has marketed himself exclusively to the
community of infertile couples, and his practice has grown accordingly. He is one of only five practices in the country that focuses

Figure 14.3   Berkley Center

solely on the fertility issue, and when he started, he was the only one for many years, which made him the "go to" person for the issue, a distinction he has retained. Another key to his success is referrals from colleagues, who know he specializes in a very specific niche.

Mike took a big risk. He never had a business plan, but he planned on doing well. His confidence and hard work, coupled with the results his patients have achieved, have been the secrets to his success. He thinks big and insists on big outcomes. He showed early signs of this entrepreneurial streak, earning money shining shoes when he was 10 years old. As an acupuncturist, he took a risk from the beginning and leased an office with a high rent and a good location with the expectation that it would work, and he is a tireless promoter of his business. He does his own public relations. He pitched his story of a Jewish guy practicing Chinese medicine in Manhattan to the press, getting great exposure. Before he even started focusing on the fertility market, Mike was hustling hard to get ahead. As he says, "I wrote letters to other doctors, I networked with therapists, you know. I can get out there and generate revenue, but I had no business plan. My plan was to wake up at six in the morning and work until nine at night and grow this thing." Mike is not satisfied with his success yet. He still wants to grow. Like most successful businesspeople I talked to, he has a sense of urgency, which is essential.

However, I don't want you to take this approach. I want you to plan for the future—even if you can't guarantee a result. I don't want you working 14 hours a day. Not even close.

Mike started as a one-man show. Now, though his business is branded with his name, he has turned his practice into a center offering complementary services delivered by other trained practitioners in various areas, including but not limited to yoga, nutrition, and mental health. Mike has combined the full-service building block and the branding building block to grow his business beyond booked solid. Once his center was successfully booked solid, he began opening other Berkley Wellness Centers, either by partnering with an existing acupuncturist and rebranding the business or by acquiring another practice altogether. Strategic alliances are one of the most important parts of his strategy.

He makes the same basic proposition to the acupuncturists with whom he wants to ally. "I want to take over your practice. I'm going to do all your marketing, I'm going to handle all your billing, all your reception duties—everything. All you have to do is show up. We'll call your business the Berkley Center for Reproductive Medicine. You're going to be the director of complementary medicine at this branch, and we'll split earnings and expenses 50/50. The reason it's going to benefit you is because at present, you're seeing 20 patients per week, and I'm going to get you up to seeing 80 patients per week." Mike is interested in partnering with small practices that aren't doing well. He shows them how he can make the practice triple and quadruple in volume. In return, he takes a piece of the receivables. As a corollary, he believes in "doing what you are good at and outsourcing the rest." He used to try to motivate people with money, but he learned that most people need to have a purpose and want to contribute to society. What a good idea!

Lori Kliman and Heather White and Cupcakes by Heather and Lori

Lori Kliman and Heather White are the owners and founders of Cupcakes by Heather and Lori, which sells retail and wholesale cupcakes, cakes, and other goodies in Vancouver, Canada. They have two stores (as of June 2007) and supply cupcakes to some of the most popular grocery stores in the area. Lori and Heather met as teenagers working in retail, and both assumed that they would have careers in the retail fashion industry as adults. Although they moved to different cities, they both ended up working for Odorchem Manufacturing Corporation, which sold Ona technology, an odor-neutralizing product. And then, as fate would have it, Lori had set up a New York distributor right before September 11, 2001, and both Lori and Heather were sent to New York to set the product up on site at Ground Zero. One day during some down time, Lori took Heather to the trendy (and, yes, delicious) Magnolia Bakery for some comforting cupcakes (full disclosure—when I lived in New York City, I indulged in more than my fair share of baked treats from Magnolia Bakery, but I get no commission if you go buy some based on my recommendation). In the cab on the way back to their hotel, cupcakes safely boxed on their laps, Heather said (out of the clear blue), "Why don't we start a cupcake bakery in Vancouver?"

Lori was happy with her job and future prospects at the time, but Heather was inspired by the concept and kept coming back to it. They mulled it over for a year until they pulled the trigger and applied for a lease on a location in Vancouver. They had no specific expectations when they started, just a business idea and the desire to make it happen. The risk was enormous when they opened their store in a high-rent, high-turnover, seasonal district. Lori says, "Everyone came in the doors the first summer seemingly just to tell us that we would be closed in two or three months. So that was discouraging, but at the same time, these people didn't realize that it gave Heather and me the strength to prove them wrong."

They borrowed the money to start the business with faith in a positive outcome. Interestingly though, neither Lori nor Heather, are bakers. They didn't see that as a problem—they simply hired bakers, who worked with them to create the ideal systems in each area of the business—and they documented every system (Figure 14.4).

According to Lori, "I never, ever thought I would learn how to bake, and so many people, in the beginning, told me you have to know how to bake if you're going to have a bakery. I couldn't understand that. I said, why? That has nothing to do with it. What I'm good at is selling and marketing and P.R. and that's what I'm going to focus on. I think that you hire people who are very good in their field, and you do what you're really good at, and ultimately, that makes you

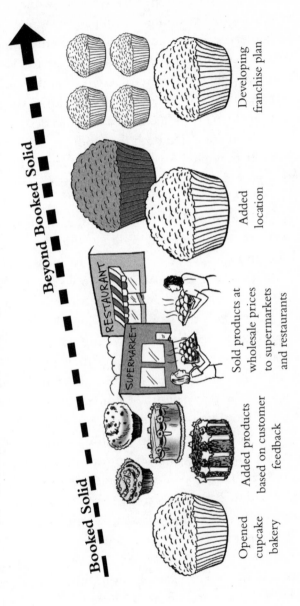

Cupcakes by Heather and Lori: www.cupcakesonline.com

Booked Solid

Opened cupcake bakery

Added products based on customer feedback

Sold products at wholesale prices to supermarkets and restaurants

Added location

Developing franchise plan

Beyond Booked Solid

Figure 14.4 Cupcakes

happy because you love what you do, and it also encourages a great environment because you have people who are working with you who love doing what they're doing." From pastry people, for example, Lori and Heather learned that in normal kitchen setups there is a boss or a superior who controls the design of the pastries. Heather and Lori gave their pastry chefs freedom to design what they wanted. Lori and Heather are terrific examples of people who knew their strengths and stayed within them. They let the bakers and designers develop the products. The staff cocreated both the products and the systems to produce the products, while Lori and Heather focused on marketing. Everyone is happy and creative. The result—a great product and little staff turnover.

Lori and Heather spread the word about Cupcakes by attending community events, giving away product, and supplying cupcakes to coffee shops and grocery stores in order to increase their brand recognition and exposure and to attract people from areas outside the store's neighborhood. They also nurtured relationships with the media, who helped spread the word about Cupcakes.

Customer feedback has been a very important metric for Lori and Heather as they improve and develop their product line. They spend a lot of time on the floor connecting with customers, and they elicit feedback at every possible moment. They are very good about measuring their initiatives and tracking their results.

Because Lori and Heather are in touch with their business metrics, they didn't rush into expansion. Instead they set milestones to hit and goals to reach. They used their customer feedback and chose their second location based, in part, on that valuable information. In order to expand, to get to the next level, they knew they would need to collaborate even more than they were used to. They were pragmatic in their approach. They researched other businesses to see how they were doing it. For example, were others creating products in a central location or at each location? They chose the best methods based on what others had found successful. How'd they find out what worked? Simple. They just called up other business owners. They also are involved in an organization for women entrepreneurs and vet their new ideas and plans through these accountability partners.

Their metrics are balanced with their urgent desire to grow. If a new opportunity arises and they feel good about it, they say yes and then figure out how to fulfill their promise. Sometimes urgency trumps research, but they try to be judicious, like the first time they had an opportunity to make wedding cakes. They went for it without first calculating all the possible outcomes. Fortunately, wedding cakes became a major part of their product line—a great example of learning in action and being flexible.

Lori and Heather plan on opening a few more locations and then offering a franchise model so others can open their own Cupcake bakeries. They'll do it, too. With the technology they use to track the important metrics of the business, such as customer spending habits and tastes, they will be able to tailor product offerings at each location and advise franchisees.

Lori and Heather don't wait around for luck to strike. They have found the balance between learning and action so they can grow the business faster and maintain a sensible pragmatic approach to strategic planning and decision making.

Brian Scudamore and 1–800–Got–Junk?

Brian Scudamore doesn't have a lot of patience for things he's not interested in. How many of us do? He dropped out of high school then later thought he'd give college a try—but he needed a way to pay for it. Sitting in a McDonald's a couple of days before he turned 19, he saw a beat-up old junk truck and thought he could pick up some extra cash by hauling away unwanted junk. Every mother's dream for their son, right? So, with $700 he bought a truck and started collecting junk. Two years later, he was doing so well he dropped out of college. He is now the CEO of 1–800–Got–Junk?, a company with revenues around $100 million (Figure 14.5).

1–800–Got–Junk? by Brian Scudamore: www.1800GOTJUNK?.com

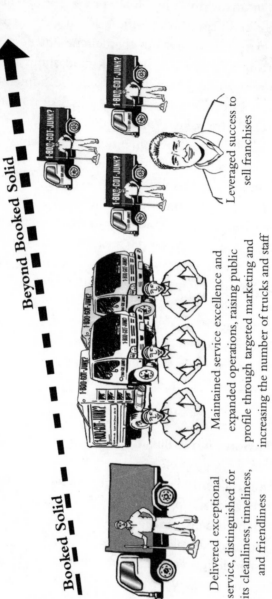

Figure 14.5 Junk

He bought more trucks and hired staff. He differentiated the company by providing clean trucks and clean drivers offering up-front fees and on-time service, features that make sense to us as possible consumers but that are not at all typical in the junk removal business. Right from the beginning Brian wanted to build something big, so he focused on systems at the earliest possible moment. As he says, "I had a philosophy that we could build something much bigger together than any one of us could build alone. By having a franchise organization with a bunch of great franchise partners who all have investments into the brand, time, energy, and money, together we could build something much greater. I put together a board of advisors in 1997/1998. We said, Okay, time to franchise. And that's the model I chose."

1-800-Got-Junk? is a marketing powerhouse. Yet, they spend very little money on marketing and get extraordinary results. They have had thousands of press mentions, from media outlets including CNN, CBS, CNBC, *Fortune,* the *New York Times, Wall Street Journal*; and, yes, they have even been on *Oprah.* Their franchisees and staff members wear big blue wigs while holding up 1-800-Got-Junk? signs and wave wildly at passing traffic. They also find strategic places to park their always clean-and-shiny, white-and-blue trucks.

1-800-Got-Junk? tracks customer service (timeliness, cleanliness, friendliness, etc.) and revenues as main metrics, has a system for creating systems, and now has a department to update and train employees and franchisees on systems. When asked whether he thinks talented people or effective systems are more important to the success of his business, Brian says, "It's 100 percent focused on systems, but those systems include finding the right people. You need the proper selection system, recruiting systems, training systems, and operational systems. If we had all these great people and all this talent, but we didn't have the systems to ensure that we can support them once they're in their roles, I think we would be in trouble." Brian believes so strongly in working with others to create a remarkable company that he has recently created a profit-sharing plan and says this has created more accountability and more of a bottom-line focus.

Brian may have started in the junk business, but he's now in the franchising business. Remember that I mentioned this earlier as something to ask yourself as you expand your business: What business am I going into?

When asked whether he would have done anything differently, knowing now what he didn't know then, he says, "I really would not have done anything differently because I believe that there's been so much learning along the way that has been critical. If I didn't learn from that one big mistake or those two big mistakes, then I might have made that same mistake at a stage in the business when the business was too big to handle the mistake. There's nothing that I would have done differently."

Jonathan Hunt and FundNet.ca

Jonathan Hunt, founder and CEO of FundNet.ca, was a seasoned financial planner with 20 years in the industry, serving clients as well as managing other planners. Though he was doing very well professionally, he decided that he wanted to make a lifestyle change. He dreamed of finding a way to take his business online, so he could travel and work from anywhere. He also wanted to build a business that was much more leveraged than serving clients in the typical financial services model. In order to do so, he knew he needed to build a better mousetrap, and Jonathan did just that.

He says, "I decided that to be able to do business online, I would need to be able to put together a communications infrastructure that would allow me to work with my clients over the Internet instead of in person. There were some significant advantages with this. First of all, if I could, I would be able to do it from anywhere. But beyond that, I would be able to communicate in a one-to-many fashion as opposed to exclusively on a one-to-one basis, which is what the financial business is typically all about. We figured out what are the core things a planner does with his clients, and it basically came down to three things: When you see clients you give them some information about what's going on in the marketplace—in other words, you give them some guidance; you give them an account statement; and then you give them some recommendations. We looked at that and said, Okay, how can we build this into a formula to take it online?"

Hunt created a new business architecture with an online service that informed and advised his clients in a timely, efficient way. It also allowed them to make online transactions based on that information. Not only that, he worked with the all-important compliance department of his company to ensure that the tools he was building had the right features to make all the marketing and financial reporting issues that compliance deals with easier and more efficient. So he figured out how to serve his clients and serve the internal compliance needs of any financial planning operation.

It's important to note that he did this when the Internet was just starting to take shape. So, it was new not only for his clients but also for him, too. Jonathan didn't have a technology background, but he saw technology as a tool that could be used in his industry and smartly predicted where the market was going. He demonstrated extraordinary flexibility, adapting to a market in flux, and he was patient as his clients caught up with the new technology.

At the beginning, Jonathan took on all the responsibilities of the business. He didn't raise any capital to fund the start-up but says that if he had to do it all over again, he would because he's found it very challenging to grow the business on cash flow alone. Because of the financial constraints, Jonathan had to take care of sales, support, customer service, and training, which inhibited the speed at which he could grow. As he says, "I was booked solid with various different service obligations as opposed to being booked solid with service revenues." Yet, he did it. He started as a financial planner—and got booked solid. He then built a better business architecture, this time online—and again got booked solid. And the new architecture is designed in such a way that he can make more money and work less (Figure 14.6).

Fundnet, Connecting Financial Advisors by Johnathan Hunt: fundnet.ca

Beyond Booked Solid

Booked Solid

Financial planner

Senior manager in financial planning firm

Developed online product to help serve his clients and to enable him to serve more clients from flexible locations, while working less

Now sells the online client services software system to other financial planners

Figure 14.6 Fundnet

Still, he's the first to admit that letting go of responsibilities has been more challenging than he thought it would be. As much as we all say we'd like to work less, few of us in the entrepreneurial world find it easy to actually do that, and not because we *have* to keep working. Jonathan believed, as do many business owners, that others wouldn't be able to perform as well as he did, and that was only part of the challenge. It took him a while to realize that he needed to set and to manage new expectations for his clients as well. He says, "After dealing with clients personally over a number of years, they want to talk to the top dog, and they can recognize when they have someone who does not have as much experience on the phone. There's not the relationship built there, so it's just way too easy to call me and ask me to do busy administrative tasks like change an address. Other challenges include trusting that you have staffing in place that is competent enough to be able to execute on the different initiatives you've got going."

Jonathan has been diligent about creating a business architecture that offers products strong enough to stand on their own, that are not dependent on him doing the work. As he was building the company, Jonathan was clear that he needed to create a scalable business; so he and his team avoided chasing one-off opportunities or situation-dependent products. He measures all business decisions against this metric. Well, almost all.

At the beginning, he was willing to take risks and learn in action. He says, "You see, we first created the software just for our clients. I hadn't planned on selling it to other financial planners at that time. Then one day, another financial planner cornered me in a bar and asked, 'If you were going to sell a system, how much would you sell it for?' Out of the blue I picked a number. I said ten thousand bucks. I got up to get a drink, and I came back and there was a check on the table for $5,000. She said, 'Here's a deposit for your first system, and I'll give you the other half when it's done.' Very shortly thereafter the president of her company called me up and said, 'I want you to come and speak at the chairman's appreciation council meeting and tell everybody what you're doing.' I did, and a bunch more checks came in. That's when I knew I had something special."

Now, instead of working with consumers, Jonathan works exclusively with other financial planners who want to buy and use his software for their clients.

Over the past few years, FundNet.ca has automated all support calls, and the company uses a software tool for project management. They track all metrics and have up-to-date data to use when making strategic decisions. They have a strong technology base; and now that they have added live data to their static systems, they are able to make timely, dynamic decisions and tweak their services accordingly. Jonathan says this is one of FundNet's greatest strengths—the relentless pursuit of new systems and tools to keep the most current and relevant tracking data.

It's great to have success. But what's it all for? What does it even mean? Well, for Jonathan it means giving back to the community. He is creating a piece of software called Giving Nation, which will allow corporations to be able to give part of their donation dollars to employees to distribute to the charities of their choice. Very nice.

Kody Bateman and SendOutCards.com

Kody Batemen founded SendOutCards.com to help people become what he calls "card senders." That's the kind of person you always wanted to be but never got around to being—someone who remembers everyone's birthday and sends a card on time, someone who sends thank-you cards to friends and business colleagues, someone who has organized tickler systems that support their business marketing efforts, and so on.

Kody has a theory that people experience what he calls "promptings," thoughts that pass through our consciousness in about a minute or less that "prompt" us to get in touch with someone. Promptings can come in the "I'm thinking of you," or "Happy Birthday," or "Thank you," or "I appreciate our friendship" variety; or they can be more prosaic, such as "I hope you're still enjoying the boat I sold you" or "I enjoyed working with you, so keep me in mind for future projects." What happens, according to Kody—and I've certainly found it to be true—is that promptings disappear from our consciousness as quickly as they come, so the result is that we rarely act on them. Kody's idea was inspired by just such an event.

In 1989, he had an internship in New York City. Newly married, with a 12-month-old baby, he was itchy to pack up his things and hit the road for the long drive from Utah to New York. As he was saying his goodbyes to his family, he noticed his brother Chris, who was four years older, moving some of their father's company trucks around. Chris worked in the family business. Kody thought he ought to take a moment to walk over to his brother to give him a proper hug goodbye and tell him that he loved him and that he was a great brother. But he didn't respond to the prompting. He was in a hurry. Three months later, Kody got a call from his mother in Utah to tell him his brother Chris had been killed. It was the first of many sleepless nights during which Kody had wrestled with the fact that he had ignored the prompting to say a proper goodbye to his brother that day three months earlier. He made a promise to his brother that not only would he not do it again, but he would do whatever he could to help other people act on their promptings.

Kody started in 1991 with a program called Personal Touch Power Systems, which was essentially a day planner designed to help people act on their promptings. Studies have shown that the average consumer buys 10 greeting cards per year; but they need 70 (yes—70), not including holiday cards. That's a lot of promptings going unanswered. The Personal Touch planner had sleeves for storing greeting cards bought the first of each month in anticipation of people's birthdays and other events you might want to send a card for.

He created 90-minute free seminars that fed into full-day seminars to train people in the system and the philosophy. The system had limitations. People still had to go to the card store. It hadn't quite removed the physical and psychic limitations that prevent people from acting on their promptings.

But Kody's dream was big, and the inspiration for his dream was powerful. He thought he was going to the moon with Personal Touch Power Systems; when it didn't work, he didn't let the setback set him back. Instead he saw that it had brought him one step closer to delivering on his promise to his brother. The next steppingstone to his dream came from a different direction. He took what at first might have seemed like a detour from his dream and started Glyphics Communication, selling telecommunication products (like long distance service and conference calling services) to network marketing companies. Between 1992 and 2002, the business grew to an $18-million-a-year operation. As a supplier to network marketing companies, Kody met with the top executives and top distributors at many of the most successful network marketing companies. He saw the enormous potential of the business architecture and thought it might apply to his dream company.

In 1999, he started an Internet version of the Personal Touch system, but it still didn't have the ability to send a physical card with the touch of a button. He started watching the digital printing industry. In 2001, he realized that the technology he needed had come together, but he needed financing. So he and his wife took a huge risk. They sold out of Glyphics and started Treat 'Em Right Solutions, a card-sending company that catered specifically to businesses. His first clients were boat dealerships (Mastercraft boats and then Malibu boats, for those of you who are boat connoisseurs) who wanted to stay in touch with customers. They would typically set up five-card campaigns that went something like this: thank you for your business; I hope you're enjoying your boat; it's time for your first "free" service; Happy Holidays; and Happy Birthday.

Although he didn't start the company as a network marketing business, he had long known that it was the architecture he would ultimately build. Over the next couple of years, he did most of the selling himself, eventually hiring eight or so independent agents. He was also building the system and building a card catalog. Then in 2003, he incorporated SendOutCards.com and got the licensing to become a network marketing company. That meant all sorts of systems on the programming and legal side. The multiple-tier pay structures, for example, require a sophisticated program to track each layer of distributor and the payout streams, what's called a genealogy in network marketing (if you think this is a building block for you, you will need to do research into the structure, which can get complicated). With a card catalog of about two hundred greeting cards, they started signing up distributors (Figure 14.7).

For the next year, Kody, his family, and his distributors worked exceptionally hard. They had presentations almost every night and meetings with businesses during the day. As Kody says, "There's so much work involved, it would scare you. In fact, there's this old adage that most entrepreneurs learn later on: *Fortunately, you learn later on*. If entrepreneurs knew the amount of work it takes to accomplish their goal of building a company, if they knew all the details before they started it, they probably never would." Kody learned to take things one day at a time, learning how to jump through each hoop as it came up.

SendOutCards.com now has more than 8,000 stock cards and the ability to create custom cards. It uses technology that enables people to send actual, physical, paper cards out from their desktop, which means no trying to find time to get to the card store, no hunting for your friend or work colleague's address for the umpteenth time, no going to the post office because you don't have stamps, no trying to remember to get the envelope in the mailbox. SendOutCards.com even has technology that enables you to create your own handwriting font so your cards look like they were written by hand. How cool is that?

SendOutCards by Kody Bateman: www.SendOutCards.com

Booked Solid

Beyond Booked Solid

Had idea for card-sending company, but no financial resources

Started Glyphics Communications, selling long distance and conference phone services to network marketing companies

Sold Glyphics and used proceeds to launch Internet card-sending company: Treat 'Em Right Solutions

Settled on network marketing business structure, which enabled consistent high quality and duplication. Renamed business SendOutCards

Engaged others to handle day-to-day operations and became teacher and trainer to better collaborate with others to build the business

Figure 14.7 SendOutCards

And the network marketing structure works wonderfully because of Kody's powerful underlying passion and because of the enthusiasm of SendOutCards.com users who in turn become distributors and so on. Users want to pass the word along. So why not make money while they're at it, signing new people up?

In 2004, he realized that the traditional network marketing compensation model didn't work for online greeting card distribution. Not only that, no one could help him design a better compensation system because no one had ever done what he was doing before. But his team worked through it and launched a better compensation plan in June 2005. The genealogy, the system used to track the compensation plan, is not the only important system in the company.

Kody believes in having systems for just about everything, from distributor kits, to training manuals, to company policies, to the rules of engagement for the customer support team. As Kody says, "We can bring in a branded customer support person and over the course of two weeks, we can not only teach them the a,b,c approach, but we can put them on the phone, 'baptism by fire' if you will, and actually have them fully up and running in that two weeks."

For the distributors, systems are important for two reasons, according to Kody. The first and by far the most important is consistency. If a distributor is consistent in his or her activities, he or she will be successful. The second thing is duplication—the ability to duplicate what you are doing. It's all about teaching yourself to leverage. SendOutCards.com also has a monthly report that tracks everything from revenue, to how many distributors signed up, to which packages they signed up, to how many people cancelled in the month and the reasons, and so on.

With all the systems in place supporting the operation and growth of SendOutCards.com, Kody was able to take on a new role in the business. He stepped away from the daily meetings and presentations and moved into an educational role, as teacher and trainer. He was able to leverage himself away from being booked solid and into a role where he was supporting the people working in the company. The best part? Kody loves teaching. The transition, which might have been difficult (giving up some day-to-day involvement and control), was made easy because he was moving into one of his core competencies and going with his passion. He's helping employees stay focused on the big picture. "The big picture is that we're delivering on a promise to my brother. The big picture is that we're going to help millions of people act on their promptings every day and change the world. And these breakdowns that happen in business sometimes are insignificant because they're little-picture stuff, and the little-picture things are the things that try to keep a big cause from happening, and when our employees get through that and they're refocused on the big picture, that helps them get through any breakdown we may have. The challenge that most companies have is that employees don't have a vision of the big picture."

It's working. In 2003, SendOutCards.com did about $100,000 of business. In 2004, it jumped to $800,000, and in 2005, to $2.8 million. Growth tripled in 2006 and is on target to triple again in 2007. The company is growing faster than any other greeting card company, and it's just getting going. As Kody points out, for most network marketing companies, the momentum threshold is 30,000 distributors. At the time I am writing this book, SendOutCards.com is at 25,000, so the real growth has yet to begin.

Is there anything Kody would have done differently building these businesses? Only one thing—believe more in the power of his own mind. "I was always a big dreamer. I always felt that I would do something big, that we would make this thing work. But there were periods over the past 18 years when my belief in my own abilities was up to par with who I was, and that's coming from a positive person. Never underestimate the power of your mind, the power of your abilities to accomplish any goal that you have in life, to stay on course every single day."

Kody is a great example of the kind of person who joins my Think Big Revolution that I've mentioned before. He has created an environment in his company that helps everyone think bigger about who they are and what they offer the world. To meet more people like Kody, visit www.ThinkBigRevolution.com. And . . . good luck, Kody!

What an amazing group of people. Mike, Heather and Lori, Ron, and Brian built totally unexpected businesses. Brandon, Jonathan, and Kody figured out how to build their businesses way beyond what others in their fields had done before. They are truly leaders in their respective businesses. Does that mean they're perfect? No way. None of us is. Perfection in and of itself would result in stagnancy and death. They are each still struggling at some level with getting certain aspects right. Ron and Mike have a ways to go on the work-life balance. Heather and Lori are just getting started. The future is theirs for the taking, but they still have work ahead. Brian, Brandon, Jonathan, and Kody will need to keep their creative energy up as their businesses plateau and require infusions of new ideas to get to the next level.

They may not be perfect, but they are each magnificent examples of taking a business beyond booked solid. When I introduced these case studies, I listed eight guiding strategies and principles that were common to all these people: openness, urgency, risk taking, mentorship, flexibility, collaboration, systems, and metrics. Now that you've gotten to know each of them better, I'll add one last guiding principle, and perhaps the most important one: a desire to serve other people. And in some cases, this desire to serve goes well beyond the imperatives of their business. It's about serving the community, helping people, being of use. If really, truly wanting to be of service is at the core of what it takes to succeed, how great is that? It's where it all comes together—*how* and *why* you will succeed—*working on your business, while working in your business, while working on yourself.* We've come full circle back to the beginning. If this is your first time through the book, loop back to the beginning and start again. But this time as you go through the book, you will be doing the work to go beyond booked solid. You will be building your new business architecture, putting your systems in place, and achieving just the right balance for you—your business, your life, your way. Wherever you are in the process, remember—it's all inside. The rest is just getting things done.

Bibliography

Adams, Douglas. *Dirk Gently's Holistic Detective Agency*. New York: Simon & Schuster, 1987.

Adler, P. S. "Building Better Bureaucracies." *Academy of Management Executive* 13, no. 4 (1999): 36–49.

Allen, David. *Getting Things Done: The Art of Stress-Free Productivity*. New York: Viking, 2001.

Alessandra, Anthony J., and Michael J. O'Connor. *The Platinum Rule: Discover the Four Basic Business Personalities and How They Can Lead You to Success*. New York: Warner Books, 1996.

Berkun, Scott. *The Myths of Innovation*. Sebastopol, CA: O'Reilly Media, 2007.

Buckingham, Marcus. *Go Put Your Strengths to Work: 6 Powerful Steps to Achieve Outstanding Performance*. New York: Free Press, 2007.

Buckingham, Marcus, and Donald O. Clifton. *Now, Discover Your Strengths*. New York: Free Press, 2001.

Carbonara, Peter. "Hire for Attitude, Train for Skill." *Fast Company*, no. 4 (August 1996): 73.

Collins, Jim. *Good to Great: Why Some Companies Make the Leap . . . and Others Don't*. New York: Harper Business, 2001.

Csikszentmihalyi, Mihaly. *Flow: The Psychology of Optimal Experience*. New York: Harper Perennial, 1991.

Drucker, Peter. *The Practice of Management*. New York: Harper Business, 1993.

Ferriss, Timothy. *The 4-Hour Workweek: Escape 9–5, Live Anywhere, and Join the New Rich*. New York: Crown, 2007.

Gerber, Michael E. *The E-Myth Revisited: Why Most Small Businesses Don't Work and What to Do About It*. New York: Harper Business, 1995.

Godin, Seth. *The Dip: A Little Book That Teaches You When to Quit (and When to Stick)*. New York: Portfolio, 2007.

Godin, Seth. *Small Is the New Big: and 183 Riffs, Rants, and Remarkable Business Ideas*. New York: Portfolio, 2006.

Goldratt, Dr. Eliyahu, and Jeff Cox. *The Goal*. New York: North River Press, 1992.

Goleman, Dr. Daniel, Richard E. Boyatzis, and Annie McKee. *Primal Leadership: Learning to Lead with Emotional Intelligence*. Boston: Harvard Business School Press, 2004.

Hansell, Saul. "Google Keeps Tweaking Its Search Engine." *New York Times* (June 2007). www.nytimes.com/2007/06/03/business/yourmoney.

Kross, Ethan, Ozlem Ayduk, and Walter Mischel. "When Asking 'Why' Does Not Hurt: Distinguishing Rumination from Reflective Processing of Negative Emotions." *Psychological Science* 16, no. 9 (September 2005): 709–715.

Leonard, George. *Mastery: The Keys to Success and Long-Term Fulfillment*. New York: Dutton, 1991.

Liker, Jeffrey K. *The Toyota Way*. New York: McGraw-Hill, 2004.

Martin, Roger. "How Successful Leaders Think." *Harvard Business Review* (June 2007). www.hbsp.harvard.edu.

May, Matthew, and Kevin Roberts. *The Elegant Solution: Toyota's Formula for Mastering Innovation*. New York: Free Press, 2007.

McAdams, Dan. *The Redemptive Self: Stories Americans Live By*. New York: Oxford University Press, 2005.

Orwell, George. *1984*. New York: New American Library, 1949.

Port, Michael. *Book Yourself Solid: The Fastest, Easiest, and Most Reliable System for Getting More Clients Than You Can Handle Even if You Hate Marketing and Selling*. Hoboken, NJ: Wiley, 2006.

Rhoades, Ann. "Hire for Attitude, Train for Skill." *Fast Company*, August 1996.

Schwartz, Barry. *The Paradox of Choice: Why More Is Less*. New York: HarperCollins, 2004.

Spinosa, Charles, Fernando Flores, and Hubert L. Dreyfus. *Disclosing New Worlds: Entrepreneurship, Democratic Action, and the Cultivation of Solidarity*. Boulder, CO: NetLibrary, 1999.

Index

About the Author

Michael Port is the author of *Book Yourself Solid*. He's been called a "marketing guru" by the *Wall Street Journal* and is a renowned public speaker. A slightly irreverent, sometimes funny, knowledgeable, compassionate, and passionate performer, Michael hits his mark every time and leaves his audiences, readers, and clients a little smarter, much more alive and thinking a heck of a lot bigger about who they are and what they offer the world.

Born and bred in Manhattan, Michael now lives in picturesque Bucks County, Pennsylvania, where, when he's not traveling, he enjoys a quieter lifestyle. You can watch videos and read Michael's blog at www.michaelport.com.